A Telling
Of A Brother And Siste

C000065434

THE LOST CHILDHOOD

by
Dr. Yehudah Nir
and
Ilana (Lala) Weinreb Levron

Mazo Publishers

The Lost Childhood

ISBN: 978-1-936778-73-7

Published by:
Mazo Publishers
Jacksonville, Florida USA
Tel: 1-815-301-3559

Jerusalem, Israel
Tel: 972-2-652-3877

Email: mazopublishers@gmail.com
Website: www.mazopublishers.com

Dedicated To Our Mother

~~

Dedicated to Ludwig by Julek

Contents

Acknowledgements

This acknowledgement must start with my sister, Lala. It is she who is the true hero in this story of our survival. Her quick wit, audacity, intelligence, and above all, her courage are the reasons why I am here to bear witness and recount the tale. Along with my mother, she was instrumental in transforming this into a story of our triumph. Kind permission to publicize her diary has been provided by the Massuah Institute for the Study of the Holocaust at Kibbutz Tel Yitzhak.

Over twenty-five years ago a chance meeting with Jack "Kuba" Mausner, the only child survivor of Grammar School in our native town, Lwów, made memory possible. I thank him for this and for the friendship we have refound since then.

I thank my wife, Bonnie, whose love and unwavering support made the writing of this book possible.

Through the many years it took for this book to find its place, my good friend Ted Dimon was an unflagging believer in its worth and necessity. I am grateful for his friendship and support.

Thanks also to Jean Rossner for her early editorial assistance.

Unless credited differently, the historical photographs we have included in this book are from the archives of Wikipedia.

In the end, all have played a part not only in creating a book but, more important, in enabling a remaining witness to give testimony to a story that must be set down.

Yehuda Nir
New York City
December 2011

Introduction

*M*aus, Art Spiegelman's celebrated Holocaust graphic novel recounting his father's painful survival, has been widely praised for the seeming wit of its metaphor: cats and mice. The Germans are the cats, the Jews who are their prey, are the mice. Yet Yehuda Nir's extraordinary memoir, *The Lost Childhood*, belies the metaphor at its root. Nature ordains that cats hunt and kill mice. In the animal kingdom, where creatures are endowed with human mind and human conscience, nature supplies the innate necessity of instinct: which is why we do not say that cats murder mice. Cats kill mice because they must. But the Germans did not mindlessly kill; through human intellect, advanced design, and evil intent they murdered, and Nir, in remembering how his father was abducted ("arrested" is the term for criminals) and shot, will never say that his father was "killed." The Germans were conscious beings, uniformly reared as Christians, and because as men and women they were equipped with mind and conscience, they did not simply kill as instinct commands, as cats kill mice. "My father was murdered." Nir forthrightly tells us, with no masquerade of misleading metaphor. He means us to understand that the Germans were responsible for their crimes and atrocities. Who will hold a cat to account?

In *The Lost Childhood*, all who were complicit in hunting Jews as prey are held to account – the German murderers, their Ukrainian accomplices, the Poles, who, in the words of one Polish slave laborer (himself a suffering victim of German oppression), exulted, "Much as I hate Hitler, we have to be grateful to him for what he has done to the Jews." The child Yehuda, and his steadfast mother and his ingenious sister, were obliged to pose as Catholic Poles not merely to escape the Germans, but to outwit the many Poles who would have been happy to expose them as Jews worthy of murder. A "Hail Mary" memorized and recited by rote could save a Jewish life.

Nir's story is crucially anomalous; though his father and aunts and uncles and many cousins were among the millions of European Jews annihilated by the German Murder machine, he stands among the very few who eluded death. At a time when it was impossible to flee, subterfuge became a means of survival: subterfuge steeped in unimaginable danger, panic, terror, quick-wittedness and raw luck. For readers who have gone stale on the Holocaust, as some are willing to admit, Nir's record of a child pursued will reawaken fresh awareness, shock, understanding and conscience.

And something else: a knowledge that there will be no forgiveness. We will forgive the cat who devours the mouse; and even the mouse, were it sentient, would be resigned to nature's scheme of tooth and claw. But the grownup Yehuda Nir, who was for nearly the whole of his anguished childhood the quarry of human predators, knows that it is not in his hands, or in his power, to grant relief to the brutish past, or to release it from contemporary judgment. He is the victor over the slosh and treacle of willed obliviousness, of the figment that an abnormal history can flower into a normal present.

On a recent visit to Poland, Yehuda Nir, a free and living Jew, was photographed under the ruse of Auschwitz's wicked banner, *Arbeit macht frei* – an idiom that Mark Twain once foretold in an indelible axiom: the true existence of evil joy. And then Yehuda Nir went to stand before a high school class of young people, and – his memory of it still secure – chanted the Paternoster. It was a lesson stronger than any schoolbook: that sixty years ago, in his native land, a little Jewish boy, desperate to live, pretended to be what he was not, so that his neighbors would not betray him.

Cynthia Ozick, 2006

Part One

The Lost Childhood

Yehuda, in his youth.

1
The Romantic Period

It all happened very fast, although not unexpectedly. The war had started only a week before, and now I was on a straw-filled cart pulled by two tired horses, a Polish peasant at the reins, running away from the Germans southeast toward Romania.

Since my ninth birthday, in March 1939, I had seen my father listening tensely to the news on the radio. We had just bought the radio, our first, a beautiful German Telefunken: but instead of listening to music (which until then we could hear only on our Victrola), we had to watch my father nervously turning the dial in search of news from abroad in any language. He knew German as well as Polish, and claimed to understand English. During World War I he had received a degree in business from the Handelsakademie in Vienna, where English was required as preparation for commercial contacts with then-powerful Great Britain. But although my father did well as a businessman, his affairs had not required contact with England; so the fact that he knew English came as a surprise to me.

Until that time I hadn't been sure of the nature of my father's business. I sensed that we were better off than many of my parents' relatives, who would admire our beautiful apartment, grand piano, and Meissen china on their rare visits to Lwów from the small towns in eastern Poland where they lived. My mother's lifestyle enhanced that image of affluence. She would spend the morning with friends in the elegant Cafe Roma, leaving me and my sister Lala in the care of our Kinderfräulein, Rosa. My mother's involvement with household affairs was limited to picking the menu for dinner and purchasing kosher meat at our local butcher. Frieda, our German maid, was in charge of the household and cooking, although Mother was an expert cook. I remember Father being criticized by my Uncle Arthur for employing an ethnic German. "I love it," Father would answer. "Don't forget, they're working for me!"

In the summer of 1939, I began to scrutinize my father, trying to find out how strong he was, how capable of protecting us in those difficult times. I listened carefully to my parents' conversation, which was often in German so that Lala and I would not understand. I'd never revealed to them that I understood German, having been taught the language by Frieda and before that by her sister Adela, who had also worked for us. I gathered that my father's business was better than ever: he was a major manufacturer of *kilims*, the most popular type of carpets in Poland during those days. He maintained a network of artisans to hand-weave the rugs, and an army of salesmen to sell them, often door-to-door, all over Poland. I began to understand how we could afford our elegant lifestyle, my mother's endless visits to the local couturiers, the car with the chauffeur we had had the summer before, my father's fur-lined cashmere winter coat with a beaver collar, his many trips abroad. I felt very safe.

That summer everyone was talking politics, but it was beyond me to comprehend the nature of the news. The names of our own Polish leaders were somewhat familiar: the chief of the armed forces, Marshal Rydz-Śmigły; the president, Ignacy Mościcki; and the foreign minister, Beck. I had also seen the streets full of patriotic slogans. One of them, "Strong, United, and Ready," we joked about at home: "Strong to retreat, united to cheat, and ready to give up." All I remember of the foreign governments of that time is the names of Chamberlain and Hitler. The name Chamberlain had a benign association for me – his perennial umbrella made

Rydz-Śmigły receiving the Marshal's baton from president of Poland Ignacy Mościcki. November 10, 1936, Warsaw.

me think of Charlie Chaplin – but Hitler sounded ominous, like the man-eating monsters in stories from my early childhood.

War, the omnipresent word of those days, was still a very abstract concept. It sounded exciting. In June, warplanes flew very low and trial air-raid warnings were broadcast on the radio; a man with a very low, frightening voice would announce, "Caution, caution; it's coming... it's coming." No doubt it was. But none of us knew what was coming, or when.

In July, we went away as usual for our summer vacation in the country, but my parents were very tense. I heard my mother telling Father, after he had refused me an additional allowance, "Let him have it; you don't know how long we will be able to afford it." I found this special permissiveness very disturbing.

Two days before the war began, we came back from the country. School was to start that week. Despite all the warnings, we were not prepared. When the first German plane attacked Lwów, the radio was playing martial music ironically appropriate to events in the air. The usual low-pitched announcer wasn't there. Sirens started to sound only after the bombing, as the planes were leaving. A week later, almost half of Poland had been overrun by the Germans; Britain and France had declared war on Germany and my parents, my sister Lala, and I were in a cart on our way to the Romanian border.

Lala's boyfriend, Lonek, and his parents had left a few days earlier. Unlike us, Lonek's parents had a car, a funny looking, beetle-like Skoda. Our horse-drawn vehicle was not unusual for those days, but in one short week we were transformed from a well-to-do middle class family into four refugees. It was the beginning of a long journey for which we were unprepared.

We must have looked funny in that cart. My father wore his custom-tailored cashmere fall coat and brown Borselino hat. He looked tense, his dark brown eyes conveying determination. His black bushy hair and large protruding nose gave him a very masculine and distinctly Semitic, Middle-Eastern appearance. Mother, on the other hand, exuded her usual ladylike calm and good spirits. She was wearing one of the beautiful, beige Chanel-like woolen suits that Mrs. Herzog, the local couturier, had made for her that spring, together with a silver fox scarf and matching hat. With her light brown hair beautifully set by the hairdresser who had come to our home that morning, her innocent blue eyes, perfect complexion, and light pink lipstick, she seemed totally out of place in this straw-filled vehicle.

My sister and I wore our Shabbos clothes, which were supposed to last the longest. We took only two suitcases with us, enough, according to my mother to tide us over until we got to Romania, where my father's sister lived and where "we should have no problems."

Yehuda and Lala's mother and father.

We were silent during the first day of the trip. I guess we were overwhelmed by our new situation, and unable to appreciate the comfort of being refugees not on foot, but in a cart drawn by horses. Six years later, in 1945, we would be barefoot, pulling a cart ourselves. Compared to our way back from Germany to Poland, this trip was a luxury cruise.

In the second week of the war, the Polish army was already on the verge of collapse. We got an inkling of the situation when we saw army trucks racing back and forth on the dirt roads, roads which were the highways of those days. Each time they were confronted with rumbling tanks our horses panicked, and we were forced off the road. As a result we covered only twenty kilometers the first day. By the end of the second day my father realized that we were not going to make it to the border. Rumor had it that the Russians had made a deal with the Germans to divide Poland in two and had invaded Poland from the east. They were said to be only kilometers from where we were to sleep that night.

We had guessed from the behavior of the Polish army that the situation was growing worse. Soldiers had stopped our cart several times during the day, searching for weapons. It was hard to believe that they could suspect us of smuggling arms. For whom would we smuggle? From where? I was rather disappointed when they didn't find a gun on my father. I was sure he had one; surely he wouldn't have taken us on such a dangerous trip without a gun to protect us.

I had always overestimated my father. When I was six he had sent me a post card from Zakopane, a winter ski resort which showed a man on skis jumping high in the air. On the other side of the card my father had written, "How do you like my progress?" This was the first time I had learned of my father's skiing or for that matter, his being involved in any sport. I was exhilarated. The card made the rounds among my school friends, and my popularity skyrocketed. Years later, after my father had been murdered, I found the picture in his desk. It was only then that I realized it was a commercial post card.

Our first encounter with the Russians came unexpectedly. We were stopped by soldiers again, but to our amazement these looked different: they had two red stars on their lapels, pointed army hats, and very dirty, smelly uniforms. It was clear that this was the Red Army, freeing Poland (so they said) from capitalist oppression. They would not search for guns, they assured us, but they did want to see our documents. My father took out his wallet. The soldier examined its contents, extracted the cash, thanked us, saluted, and left. We were stunned. Rookie refugees, we were not used to such treatment. My father was shaking; he wanted revenge. The Polish coachman, being more realistic, suggested we move on. A few minutes later we encountered a group of Soviet officers. Despite Mother's objections, my father self-righteously stopped to complain. Supporting himself with one hand on the side rail, he jumped off the cart. Then he crossed over to the army truck and exchanged a few words with one of the officers who had reached out to help him climb onto the truck platform. Within seconds, he had driven off with the officers. He returned a short while later, waving a sheaf of bills at us. The Soviets had taken my father back to the soldier who had our money, told Father to take back what was his, and returned him to us. He boasted that he had taken double what belonged to him. We believed him then.

Our exile from Lwów lasted all of ten days. A week after we had encountered them, the Russians met their German counterparts halfway through Poland. Lwów became part of the Soviet Ukraine, and we returned home. It was a pleasant surprise to find or apartment just as we left it, our maid Frieda still there, our property untouched. If I could divide the war into stages or periods, this would have been the age of the innocence, the romantic period. Properties were still respected, ownerships honored, belongings returned. This phase was not to last long.

In November the Soviets pronounced my father a "capitalist," as he owned a factory and the apartment house we lived in. We were ordered to move to a smaller apartment in our building and, later on, to sublet a room in that apartment to a young Russian officer and his wife. The Russians took over Father's factory and told him to get a job as a bookkeeper. This change of status overwhelmed him. He became subdued and paced restlessly through the apartment, impatient for the evening, when he could tune in the radio, shortwave reception of foreign stations being better at night. Although temporarily safe from German occupation and concentration camps, he knew how precarious his position was. As a "capitalist" he would probably be deported to Siberia; as a Jew he was doomed in Germany. The Romanian border, our only gate to freedom, was sealed off. He felt trapped. My Romanian uncle sent a messenger with plans for an illegal crossing of the border, but we feared a trap or blackmail.

My father's weakened position in the outside world somehow demoted him from the role of paterfamilias at home. Suddenly my mother took on new importance. She became the backbone of the family, a role she was to maintain throughout much of the war. While often sad, she never seemed frightened or helpless. I sensed the determination behind her low-keyed, somewhat passive stance. It was always either yes or no, with very little ambivalence – an attitude that would help us to make quick decisions in situations where our lives depended on an ability to act immediately. It was an important ability to have in those days. She was also very busy with household chores, as our maid and my governess were gone. She spent her free time knitting sweaters, which she then sold to stores. She knitted silently, listening to Father's daily analyses of the political situation.

The situation at home was very painful for me. But in school I was having a wonderful time. Hebrew, a language not recognized by the Russians because it was used by the Zionists, was replaced by Yiddish, and then a few months later by Ukrainian, with Russian as the second language. By the time I was ten, I spoke five languages. But more than that, the school atmosphere was exhilarating. New equipment, labs, toys, and books poured in as from a horn of plenty. The Soviets believed in starting their indoctrination early; they lavished attention on us children. The local count's palace was turned into a youth center, and we were asked to join the Pioneer movement, the Soviet equivalent of Boy Scouts. I felt like a double agent. I knew I didn't belong at the youth group meetings: I was the son of a capitalist. At home, I kept wondering why my parents couldn't forget their past and enjoy life as I did. Of course, I didn't voice any of these thoughts.

Ludwig, our next-door neighbor, was my only confidant. He shared my opinions.[1]

The conflict between my experience at home and my experience in the outside world kept growing in intensity. In retrospect, I can see that this identity split was good preparation for what was to follow. At the time, however, I was torn between the fun of my school experience and extracurricular activities and the acute pain and sadness of my parents.

The Soviets relentlessly fed us propaganda about Russia, Stalin, and the Soviet system. To my ten-year-old mind, Stalin was a benign, grandfatherly hero. We were shown pictures of him embracing children for outstanding patriotic deeds. He had kissed Mamlakat, a little girl from the Republic of Uzbekistan, for picking more cotton than any girl her age. If only cotton were cultivated near Lwów! Then I could compete with her! As it was, I had to find another hero.

I didn't have to wait long. A new Soviet story or poem was read to us each week. My next hero was Volodya, a boy my age who one day noticed a time bomb the White Russians had placed on the railroad tracks. Volodya took off his red tie – the "Galstock" of the Pioneer Youth Movement and waved it vigorously, stopping a train a few feet from the bomb. For weeks afterward, I waved my red Galstock in my parents' bedroom, stopping scores of imaginary trains.

My father's early apprehensions were well founded. In the second year of the occupation of Poland, the Soviets started arresting formerly well-to-do businessmen and deporting them and their families to labor camps in Siberia. People were herded into freight trains in the dead of winter. Without adequate heat or food they traveled for many days, and even weeks, to labor camps. I heard many horror stories about those transports, as several of my parents' friends were taken.

My father was saved from deportation by a fluke. The Soviets took Mr. Mett, the manager of his company, under the impression that Mr. Mett was the owner. We did not discover the mistake for six months, and my father spent that entire time in hiding. It was an odd sort of hiding. For their own peculiar reasons, the KGB made arrests only at night. My father could still work during the day as a bookkeeper and have dinner at home, but he left around eight o'clock in the evening, slept at a friend's house, and returned to us early the next morning. I was given a special assignment: each morning I hung a white towel out the window as a sign for my father that the police weren't waiting for him and he could safely

---

1   See Part Two; Lala's Story, *Ludwig Zelig – A Memoir*

return. For weeks everything went smoothly. Then one morning my father didn't show up. At first we thought he had overslept, but when he wasn't back by nine we knew something was wrong. He must have been arrested at his friend's house. I was sure I would never see him again. Early that afternoon, the friend called: I had forgotten to hang out the usual white towel that morning; my father, assuming that the police were waiting, had returned to his friend to hide.

The Soviet occupation was my first exposure to the world of the unpredictable. Everything around me was full of contradictions. Within the limitations of a ten year old mind, I had to try to make sense of it all. My father, for example, was a bookkeeper for a government-operated company during the day, and a criminal in hiding at night. I myself, the son of a capitalist, was promoted to unit leader in my Soviet Pioneer group. And while the Soviets claimed to have come to liberate us from capitalist oppression and deprivation, it was obvious that they themselves were most deprived: within weeks of their arrival, they had emptied our stores. They were particularly obsessed with *chasy* – watches and clocks; the Russians had not manufactured watches since 1918, and the soldiers bought or confiscated every watch in sight. Some of them could be seen wearing three on each wrist. We heard anecdotes of soldiers asking watchmakers to make several small watches from one big clock, or of enterprising street vendors selling empty watch cases to the Russians, faking the tick-tock sound by knocking a fingernail gently on the case while holding it against the potential buyer's ear. It was confusing to see our conquerors as naïve, gullible children. Were they really childlike? Or were we just trying to neutralize their threat by seeing them as naïve and vulnerable?

I seemed to be the only one in my family trying to resolve such contradictions. Lala couldn't have cared less, and I envied her. She reduced the number of her suitors to two. Ludwig, at nineteen, was the embodiment of intellectualism: a university student whose first book which he had not only written, but also had illustrated with his own photographs, was about to be published. The first one-man show of his paintings was just over and Lala was the subject of about eighty percent of the canvases. But this wasn't enough for her. She needed someone to reflect the physical aspects of the world. Enter Sigmund, the basketball star. Having strengths in completely different areas, Ludwig and Siggy did not resent each other. They may have realized that, like the suitors in Truffaut's Jules and Jim, they complemented each other. A year later, during the German occupation, when Ludwig used his artistic talents to produce false documents, he made one for Siggy.

My parents were too preoccupied with thoughts of survival to be bothered by the absurdities of our existence, or my feeble attempts to cope with it all. The radio became the focus of their existence, particularly for my father. It was his periscope on a rapidly sinking submarine. The opening sounds of a BBC newscast appropriately, the first four notes from Beethoven's Fifth, "Fate" symphony, silenced all conversation. Following the news were the commentators, consistently wrong in their predictions. Only after their last words would my father turn down the radio and voice his own opinions. He always had an audience: my mother; the Madame De Farge of World War II (she could by then finish a pullover in two days); Father's older brother Schmerl, a nice man; Dr. Landau, the lawyer, who said little but did so eloquently, his erudite sentences interspersed with Latin proverbs.

There were two more members of the circle that met almost nightly at my parents' home: Mrs. Margosches, a wealthy, simple hausfrau, who was ignored, and Leon, my father's cousin from his hometown, Kolomyja. Young, tall, and handsome, Leon was respected for his blue-collar common sense. He had grown up in a small community, and spoke a mixture of Polish and Yiddish. I had a feeling that my father saw Leon, twenty years his junior, as a son. There was a definite affinity between them. Being a product of different times, I was more distant from my father than Leon. I reflected a later, more worldly period in my father's life – his marriage to my mother. Leon, on the other hand, smelled of home; the shtetl where my father grew up and to which he remained emotionally attached despite his move to the big city and his attendance at the university in Vienna, his interest in Schopenhauer, his travels abroad, his success. Perhaps the closeness between the two was inspired by my father's unconscious intuition that he would not live to see his real son grow up. But this intimacy with Leon was something I resented and felt cheated by.

I was very proud of my father's central position in the political discussions and of the fact that the meetings took place in our home. All this intensified my father's importance in my eyes. I guess I had to clutch at straws: at heart I knew how precarious his position was. There were always new signs of the changed world around us. First came the change in the way he dressed. Gone were the impeccably hand-tailored suits and coats made of fine British woolens that he had brought back from abroad. The Borselino hat and the beaver collar of his fur-lined winter coat were too obvious signs of his bourgeois past to be worn these days. Gone, too, was his leather attaché case from Hermès. It was replaced with a folding macramé shopping bag, which he carried for marketing on his way home from work.

We all carried these shopping bags folded in our pockets because of the way the Russians distributed food. While there wasn't really a food shortage, there was certainly chaos in the supply system. Stores were either totally empty or crammed full of one or two items. Out of the blue a truck would pull up and deliver, say five tons of sugar to a local grocery store. If you saw such a delivery you automatically ran to the store to stand on line, and only on line did you ask what they were unloading. Then, no matter what it was – sugar, kasha, salt, or potatoes you bought the largest amount allowed for one person whether you needed it or not. It might be six months before sugar or salt would be delivered again. This method of shopping in sporadic bursts worked well enough until the summer day when the Soviets received a trainload of Romanian watermelons – our first watermelons in almost two years. By some kind of logistic miracle or nightmare, they were delivered to all the stores on the same day. All of us – my mother, my father, my Uncle Schmerl, Cousin Sidia, and I bought gigantic watermelons that day which, for lack of space we had to store in the bathtub. We never laughed so hard again during the war.

I find it difficult to picture my mother during the first two years of the war. But I clearly remember her photograph taken in the Zaleska Studio a few months before the war broke out. She was strong. Although alarmed like the rest of us by the events around us, she maintained the basic structure of the family, giving all of us badly needed physical and moral support.

The news on Father's radio was very bad. Europe was being overrun by the Nazis. The French Maginot Line I had heard so much about before the war proved to be an empty fortress against the massive power of the well-disciplined Germans. I remember asking myself in the spring of 1941 why we didn't run. It was obvious that we wouldn't be on the periphery of the war much longer. We could all sense that Russia was Hitler's next target. The tension was unbearable. What strikes me as funny, as I look back, is the feeling that Stalin must have been less in touch with the situation than I was. Why else would the Soviets have been so unprepared when the Germans attacked in June 1941?

News of the attack caught me at a friend's house downtown. It was like September 1939: air-raid sirens, people running for shelter in different directions, sources of reliable information that totally contradicted all the others. Because of the usual Russian secretiveness, the first news of the attack came from BBC. The Germans were just a few kilometers away from Lwów, and caught by surprise, the Russians were retreating in a disorganized panic.

For this last piece of information we didn't need the radio. German planes were flying low over the city, and Russian soldiers were shooting at them with rifles and pistols. Yes, with pistols. They didn't even have trucks or tanks in which to run away. Small units of the Red Army could be seen marching rapidly, often in opposite directions. The few army trucks available were ten or fifteen years old. Having broken down almost immediately, they lay abandoned in the streets. It was obvious to us that the Russians were in worse disorder than the Polish army in 1939. At age eleven I was already an expert on war.

At first my father considered fleeing with the Russians, but their disorganization made it obvious that such action was out of the question. There was also a new

The Polish Army surrenders to the Germans.

development that forced us to stay at home. Suddenly it was unsafe to leave; shots were being fired on the streets. We thought that it was the Germans gunning down the fleeing Soviets. But in fact it was the Ukrainians helping the Germans to conquer the city. Lwów had become part of the Ukraine during the Soviet occupation, and its name had been changed to Lviv, but many of the Ukrainians were fiercely anticommunist. At the first sign of Russian weakness, they had joined the ranks of the German Nazis.

The shooting stopped two days later. The streets became empty and quiet. We knew then that the Russians had left Lwów – less than two years after their occupation had begun. Although we were not sorry to see them go, we had no reason to rejoice. From the day the Russians had come, it was inevitable that the Germans would eventually force them out. For us it was only a question of when.

2
The Triumvirate

The Germans entered a week later, on June 30, 1941, my mother's thirty-eighth birthday. They were busy chasing the Russian army and left the policing of the city to their local friends the Ukrainians, who went at it with vengeance. Within days the Ukrainians had organized a police force and started arresting Jewish men on the street and sending them to the city jails. My Uncle Schmerl was among the first arrested, but he escaped several days later while being transferred to another prison. Although he had been in jail for only two days, his stories were full of terror. This was my first direct encounter with Nazi brutality, and I was overwhelmed with fear. Schmerl returned bruised, haggard, *changed.* With mounting apprehension, we listened to his horrifying tales of the abuse he had experienced, the innocent people he had seen killed, the conditions in jail.

After listening to Schmerl, my father ordered a "total alert." None of us, especially the men, were to leave home. My mother was now officially in charge. If food was available, she or I would do the shopping. Lala was not to go out; she would be easy prey for the Germans or the Ukrainians. No one talked about it, but we all felt that our days were numbered. We were trapped, afraid to leave our third-floor apartment.

The Germans' first decree required all citizens to turn in their radios with in twenty-four hours. Disobedience would be punished with death by hanging. This order put an end to our contacts with the outside world, our only source of moral support and strength. Together, my mother and I carried our Telefunken radio to the police station. My father watched us silently, his sad, deep brown eyes telling his feelings. He tried to crack a smile of encouragement when we awkwardly lifted the large box, but the smile didn't materialize. He looked about to cry. We were carrying out a part of him.

This was probably the last week of my father's life. The German army was preoccupied, probably overwhelmed by the ease of its victory on the front, and was not interfering with the attacks of the Ukrainian police on the Jews. This was not yet the era of the "Final Solution," but the Germans were pleased to give the Ukrainians – originators of pogroms, virulently anti-Semitic since the seventeenth century – a free hand. It was a green light for murder. The Ukrainians were aware that this was only a temporary arrangement, that the Gestapo would take over as soon as the Germans caught up with the moving front, so they had to hurry. Hundreds of Jews were rounded up daily, marched to the woods, and executed with machine gun fire. We had been aware of the police brutality since my uncle's arrest, but we did not know about the mass executions until much later. The bloodbath reached its climax on "Petliura Day."[1] When the police came for my father and my uncle that morning, we hoped that it was just a temporary arrest. My father didn't resist, and I followed him to the local police precinct where all the Jews were being held. Two hours later the police came for my mother. She was lying on the living-room couch, sad but not crying. When the Ukrainians arrived, she refused to go, claiming to be ill. "You'll have to carry me out if you want me," she said. Had she said this a year later,

they would have shot her on the spot, but in July 1941, their procedures of arrest were in disarray and they let her stay.

My mother's passive resistance on that day was a decisive factor in my surviving the war. Had she gone with them, I would have never seen her again. The police were back an hour later to take Lala. This, however, was for a specific assignment – to wash the toilets at the police station. I was ignored; I guess they couldn't figure out what to do with an eleven-year-old

Symon Vasylyovych Petliura boy.

1   On July 25, 1941, Ukrainian nationalists organized the next pogrom in Lwów – the so called "Petliura Days" (named after Symon Vasylyovych Petliura (picture above), one of the leaders of Ukraine's unsuccessful fight for independence, who organized anti-Jewish pogroms in this country. After WWI he was killed by a Jew in France). During the "Petliura Days" nearly 2,000 Jews were killed in Lwów.

Ukrainians drag a Jewish man down a street in Lwów, July 1941, during the Petliura Day pogrom.

Worried about my father, I followed Lala to the local precinct. My mind was racing. I was overwhelmed by the rapid flow of events. My father and my uncle arrested, my mother sick and resisting the police, my sister washing toilets for the police – what would come next? As we approached the building, I spotted a column of men, six abreast, marching out of the police yard surrounded by Ukrainians with submachine guns. My father was next to his brother in the row before the last. Our eyes met. He seemed surprised to see me on the street, and didn't notice Lala.

I followed the column for a little while. Father turned around once more and gave me a faint smile, like the one I had seen on his face a week before when we carried out the radio. I waved to him, but failed to catch his eye. One of the policemen noticed, however, and, aiming the submachine gun at me, forbade me to follow the column. I stood in place for several minutes until the prisoners were gone.

I would never see my father again.

With tears rolling down my cheeks, I slowly returned home. Lala came back late in the afternoon, exhausted and frightened. She had seen all the people at the station who were arrested with my father, and she had witnessed the brutal treatment they received. She had heard the first rumors about my father's fate: the men were being loaded on freight trains and sent to a coal mine in Austria. These rumors, with some variations, persisted for many months. Hundreds of Jewish men had been apprehended on Petliura Day, and their families had no information on their whereabouts. Later we found out that the Ukrainians had walked the men to a forest near Lwów called Piaskowa Gora, lined them up, and executed them with machine guns. My father had been murdered the day he was arrested.

But for years we didn't know whether my father was dead or alive. We thought of him not as dead, but away. I had recurrent dreams of his return, of accidentally meeting him on the street or on a train. My father never died; he just faded away, was carried off into nowhere. It was as if he were dead and alive at the same time. Even after the war, in 1945, when we found out that he had definitely been killed on the day of his arrest in July 1941, we continued to search for him through the Red Cross.

With Father's arrest, our lifestyle changed rapidly. The leader was gone and the surviving members of the family unit had to reshuffle their positions. Leading was not my mother's style; she chose instead to be the senior member of a triumvirate. From then on, decisions were made jointly, based on available information and alternatives for action. Age and experience did not matter, since we were all new to this brutal game of survival.

Although not formally designated, our roles were based on individual attributes and skills. Lala's strengths were intelligence, age, charm, and wit. My mother's strength was her gentile appearance – blondish hair, blue eyes, fair skin – along with her composure and common sense. My main asset was my age. As proven on Petliura Day, at eleven I was less noticeable than adults. I was a child and could dissolve into the background. Also, my common sense was accepted by my mother and Lala on the basis, I think, of "*vox populi, vox dei.*" Mine were instinctual, animalistic, gut reactions, uncontaminated by age, maturity, or experience and worth listening to when on the run.

Soon after Petliura Day things calmed down. The Germans took over the administration of the city, the Ukrainian police were assigned regular patrolling duties, and for a short while life was again more or less normal. With the "Final Solution" still on the Berchtesgaden drawing boards, the Germans seemed to have given us a moratorium. In reality, however, they were preparing for the final death blow by registering all Jews and by evicting Jewish families and concentrating them in one slum area that was to become the ghetto. We were allowed to stay in our apartment for the time being, and the Germans assigned us a tenant to replace the Russian officer.

Johan Kedves, a rather unusual officer of the SA (a lesser-known division of the SS), moved in with us in November 1941. I am still puzzled as to why they did not give him the whole apartment and kick us out. It must have been the major's own uneasiness about being a Nazi conqueror that made him play the role of an army officer temporarily assigned to living quarters requisitioned from a local family. Tall, blue-eyed, with reddish-blond hair, always impeccably dressed, wearing white gloves, he was the Eric von Stroheim of Renoir's *La Grande Illusion* brought to life – the very image of a perfect gentleman.

Major Kedves took the living room, the nicest in the apartment, for himself. The room was beautifully furnished, spacious, and bright, a combination living and dining room. It was dominated by the large hand-carved mahogany dining table and eight upholstered chairs where my father had held his "cabinet meetings." On the left was a matching credenza, and to the right a leather couch. Between the table and the bay windows was a grand piano, the place of Lala's martyrdom (she hated piano lessons) and our torture (we had to hear her playing while, for lack of a metronome, her teacher Mrs. Ginsburg stamped her foot rhythmically).

Major Kedves liked the room, but expressed surprise that there was no carpet and that the credenza was without bibelots. He was partial to fine china, he said, preferably Meissen. The fox must have sensed that we had hidden everything valuable. My mother, out of naiveté, or perhaps a wish to appease him, brought out the beautiful gray-and-red Kerman carpet and the porcelain figurines the major needed to "feel at home." Kedves was friendly to us throughout his stay.

We were now spending the days in the major's room, the only room in our apartment to be heated, as coal was supplied by the German army. On several occasions Kedves warned us when the Gestapo was planning an "action" (the word used at that time to describe several days of continuous arrests by the Germans) and allowed us to stay in his room. The prisoners were either executed locally or taken to concentration camps like Auschwitz, Treblinka, and Majdanek. We could see the pattern developing. Every month or so, the Gestapo took ten to fifteen percent of the city's Jewish population for extermination. It seemed that at this rate, even if we were the last to go, we had no more than a year to live. Strange though it may seem, we were not in despair; without any good reason, we felt that we would survive.

Between the "actions," life was bizarrely normal in its abnormality. We learned to live from crisis to crisis, from one life-threatening situation to the next. The days in between seemed isolated from what happened before or after. There were no newspapers or telephones. Schools were closed for all the Polish children, Christians and Jews alike. With an 8:00 p.m. curfew, our social life was cut to the minimum. Just a few visits for an exchange of the latest news or rumors in the early afternoon.

I spent most of my time foraging for food. There was no local money in circulation, and German marks were unobtainable; barter was the only means of procuring food. The peasants would bring potatoes, kasha, and barley to the local marketplace a little at a time, and wait there for people to make deals with them. Provisions were hidden under the straw of their horse-drawn wagons. They were in no hurry to negotiate, for with their peasant shrewdness they realized that we needed them more than they needed us.

A typical deal would start with "what do you have?" The answer might be "Nothing" or it might be "Eggs," depending on whether they liked one's looks or not. This would be followed by "and what do you have? Sheets?" Sheets, shirts, towels, jackets, pants, shoes – all our belongings were for barter. The problem was, how many eggs was a sheet worth? How did you assess your belongings? What would you do when all your sheets were eaten up as scrambled eggs? All this had to be weighed against the value other people placed on their sheets. I enjoyed my daily dealings, often feeling that I had outwitted the dumb peasants. In reality they were carting off everything we owned. Concert grand pianos were exchanged for sacks of potatoes. The peasants used the piano as troughs for their cows. One not-so-funny joke was about two peasants comparing the merits of a Bechstein grand to those of Steinway – for use as troughs. We had to joke about it to survive.

My mother's cousin Sidia, the Berlin-educated violinist, was evicted from her apartment and came to live with us. At this point space was not an issue. An extra cot in the bedroom was all that was needed. I found her fascinating, different from all the other people I knew. (Sidia's outlook on life combined Dadaist comic cynicism with Rilke's romantic lyricism.) She believed that, with few exceptions, all people, including the Germans, were basically good. Material objects, appearance, anything physical, was of little importance to her. She would wear my father's dark green winter coat, which came almost down to her ankles. Since we didn't have enough blankets (I had bartered most of them away during the summer), Sidia would put a heavy suitcase atop her freezing feet. It was weight, she said, not fabric that kept people warm. At mealtimes she ate only one dish, a sort of soup containing all the nutrients she considered necessary for survival. She would boil a small piece of meat or fish, throw in a vegetable or potato if any was available, and add an egg. Despite my respect for Sidia, I could never bring myself to taste this concoction. Sidia's non-conformist views permeated all aspects of her life. She claimed that women should do equal work with men and decided rather arbitrarily to become a diamond dealer on the black market in Lwów. In those days, diamonds and gold were the high-level commodities, exchanged for each other or for American dollars when those were available. I don't think there was ever a better educated or a more unlikely diamond dealer.

My mother's jewelry – a few diamond rings and a gold bracelet – had been buried by my Uncle Schmerl in the cellar of our building. We decided to dig them out and let Sidia exchange them for gold coins that were easily marketable. Late at night, unnoticed by our neighbors and concierge, I went to the cellar with Mother; she carried a candle and I took a shovel. Three hours of frantic digging produced nothing. To this day I don't know what happened. Did my uncle not bury the jewelry? Did we dig in the wrong place? Is it still there? This was a very bitter pill for us to swallow. It meant no money for the rest of the war, no funds to buy freedom or a hiding place.

A woman selling armbands in the Warsaw Ghetto (Yad Vashem).

In the autumn of 1941, we were told to wear white armbands with the blue Star of David on them. From then on, the need to find a hiding place was foremost in our minds. I felt very vulnerable on the street with the armband on and went out as little as possible. This meant less food for all of us, but it was safer, so no one minded.

Ludwig, an acquaintance, looked very Aryan: blond, blue-eyed, and a fair complexion, he decided not to wear the Star of David. Using his skills as a painter-draftsman, he made false documents attesting to his being a Catholic. The idea was simple, but it required great skill in execution. Those were the days before Xerox, and photostats were not available because of a film shortage during the war. To make a copy of a document, one had to type all its information on a sheet of paper and take the original and the typed sheet to a notary, who, upon reading both, would confirm the copy as an authentic representation of the original. Ludwig engraved his own notary stamp and typed a copy of a nonexistent baptismal certificate. With this document, he went to the police station to obtain an ID card, the Kennkarte that every gentile was expected to carry. He claimed the church where he was baptized had been burned down during the fighting, and that he could not retrieve the original.

Equipped with a Kennkarte, Ludwig went to work as a manager of a local shoe company. He spent all his free time with his cousin Rudolph, a professional photographer, preparing false papers for his relatives and friends. His method became increasingly sophisticated. For my mother and sister he followed a different scheme. Over a period of time, he surreptitiously elicited from his gentile friends detailed information as to their place and date of birth, the names of their parents, and so on. Then, without their knowledge, he wrote to the churches that kept their baptismal certificates and, claiming to be them, asked for new certificates. These were the best papers – authentic documents.

There were also blank baptismal certificates created by local clergy for sale on the black market. Ludwig would fill out a name, forge the stamp, and achieve a good semblance of the original. Their disadvantage lay in the fact that the police could check with the church and find out that no one by that name had ever been baptized. They were better, however, than notarized copies because they had an authentic look.

Ludwig was the only one of our acquaintances actually to use his papers in Lwów. The rest of us, including his mother and sister (his father, like mine had been assassinated on Petliura Day), were only beginning to contemplate a change of identity. We were scared to take this very dangerous step, and by waiting around to be forced into the decision, we almost missed our chance.

The situation was growing worse from day to day. The number of surviving Jews was shrinking rapidly with each "action." Major Kedves moved out in the winter of 1942, taking with him all our furniture: the piano, Persian carpets, china, everything. He said he had become sentimentally attached to the beautiful furniture, praised again my mother's exquisite taste, and promised to return everything when the war was over. He played the role of a gentleman to the very end. Was he so believable, or were we just so eager to believe in the possibility that we would still be alive at the end of the war? I followed the horse-drawn furniture van in order to learn his new address.

We needed money desperately. With the major gone, we rented his vacant room to a Polish couple, the Nowickis. The wife, Halina, was in about her eighth month of pregnancy. Her husband Wladek worked long hours as a plumber; I remember him only vaguely. We had nothing in common except poverty and hunger. Food, now very, very scarce, consisted mostly of potatoes. We could barely heat one tiny room, and often burned furniture in the small iron stove. Halina had no heat in her room at all. She spent hours in our rooms telling long stories of her immediate past. Spellbound, I listened to every word she said. Halina must have been in her late teens, yet she had already been married for four or five years. She had married, she said, because she didn't like her strange sounding Lithuanian maiden name, Skrybyło. She had been pregnant five times before, and had had five miscarriages. My mother, for once calling attention to my presence, tried to discourage Halina from going into all the details, but to no avail. I was mesmerized, excited and frightened all at once. I thought her life fascinating, and I admired her determination. For whatever personal reasons, she wasn't giving up. She was pregnant again, and filled with the hope of bringing a new life to the world. For the first time since my father's arrest, *I* felt some hope again.

Several days later, I was awakened in the middle of the night by Halina's screams. She was in labor. My mother rushed to her room to help her deliver. Because of the curfew, her husband Wladek could not get the midwife. After listening for a while, I fell asleep again to the sound of her screams. In the morning my mother told us that Halina had given birth to two stillborn babies. I didn't say a word.

It was very cold, a typical Polish winter. The streets were covered with deep snow, the tree branches barely holding the frosty burden. Since there was no transportation to the cemetery, it was impossible to bury the babies. We kept them frozen on the kitchen balcony until it got warmer. Halina was very sick with Puerperal fever and was bleeding again.

With the food scarcity and the freezing temperature, we often wondered if we would survive the winter. It seemed that our existence, our hopes, our expectations were in a state of continuous flux. If not daily, then at least once a week we would assess our chance of survival but often without expressing it as such. A statement "I think Mrs. X died of starvation" would imply that the food shortage was very serious: we might be next to go. "They are taking old people and children" meant anyone in that age group was in danger, if not today, then tomorrow.

These indirect, often obscure statements became our new vocabulary of danger, a method of communication that kept us all on the alert and eventually assisted us in developing survival strategies. I worried a great deal about my father. How could he stand the cold, wherever he was? My mother assured me that the climate in Austria was milder, and that it was warmer in the coal mines than above ground. During World War I, her family had escaped their estate on the Polish-Russian border, and as a child she had spent the war years in Vienna. My mother's stories from that period of her life had never meant much to me before. But now, in the midst of a new war, her tales of surviving the last one were suddenly important, almost fascinating. Compared to our experiences, hers of World War I seemed like fairy tales. My mother had attended school regularly.

Mother, Lala, and I were now spending almost all of our time together. We all slept in my parents' double bed. Gently, almost without perceiving it, we were merging into a single unit, an interdependent triangular symbiosis. Our survival was posited on this mutuality, which was both physical and emotional.

My mother's stories from the past gave me a feeling of continuity, of belonging. She was very proud of her long lineage of famous rabbis, the Hagers, who were already prominent in the sixteenth century in Eastern Europe. She was not the same woman who, just a year ago, had passively accepted my father's pronouncements in silence. Now she was a lioness, devoted to our survival. Of her stories, I liked best those dealing with shrewdness, with ways to outwit others. The one I recall most vividly was about Captain Dr. Maximillian Schleicher, who had been assigned to the traveling draft board as a physician during World War I. Not very loyal to Emperor Franz Joseph, but eager to make money, Dr. Schleicher was willing to take bribes for declaring people unfit for His Majesty's armed forces. Whenever his draft board arrived in a small town with a large Jewish population, the good doctor went to the local synagogue and announced to the rabbi that he had come to pray because he had yahrtzeit (the anniversary date of his mother's death). Within hours, the whole Jewish community would know that the army doctor was a Jew, and he would be in business. My mother's tales symbolically replaced the lessons for my bar mitzvah which was never to take place. Not yet twelve, I was already inducted into the ranks of grown men, the only one left to carry our name.

In the spring of 1942, we were told to move to the area that was to become the ghetto. The Germans started to build walls around it, but the work moved surprisingly slowly. As it turned out later, they had never intended to build a ghetto in Lwów; their idea was rather to corral the Jews into one area in order to facilitate their transport to the concentration camps. The Nazis planned to eliminate three million Polish Jews; apparently the logistics of the operation required the arrests to be staggered, each wave containing a percentage of the Jewish population in each city.

The move was painful. We took no furniture except a bed, a table, and three chairs. We were given a one-room shack with an outhouse. I hadn't known that slums like this existed in Lwów. Tiny two- and three-room houses were now divided into one-room units. Streets were unpaved; open sewage flowed in the gutter. We were among the last to come to the ghetto. We suspected that Major Kedves had put in a good word for us, so that we had been allowed a longer stay outside the ghetto walls. In fact the delay was probably accidental, but we needed to feel we had someone to protect us.

Among the people we knew, the only ones that had such protection were my Aunt Sonia and her husband Arthur, my mother's brother.

Sonia was the most talked-about member of the family. At twenty-five, she had received her Ph.D. in geology from the University of Vienna, an almost unbelievable feat for a woman in the 1930s. A few years later, she had headed a department in the Polish Petroleum Agency, another unprecedented achievement, especially for a Jewish woman. When the Russians occupied Lwów in 1939, Sonia had sequestered herself in her bedroom. For two weeks, she had left the room only to have her meals. When she reappeared, she was fluent in Russian.

I don't know why she married Arthur. He was unassuming, soft-spoken, and very sophisticated, but he had no college degree. He was usually unemployed, and except for some bookkeeping for my father, he divided his time between playing chess, reading Dostoyevsky, and taking care of their six-year-old son, Julek. Tall, balding, and fair-skinned, with beautiful eyes behind frameless spectacles, Arthur resembled a country doctor in a Chekhov play. He was just three years my mother's senior, but since the death of their father when she had been six, my mother had seen Arthur as a father figure. She always had excuses and apologies for Arthur's lack of formal education, professional training, and desire to work. It was his frail health, TB, in his teens, that had kept him from doing well, she had said to my father, who looked down on him.

Sonia was my father's favorite, the symbol of success, a self-made woman. To him, my mother and Arthur, with their aristocratic rabbinical pedigree, were dreamers incapable of facing the realities of life. "Whenever I have to make an important business decision," my father would say, "I consult Arthur and do the opposite of what he advises."

The Germans appreciated Sonia's unique talents as much as the Poles and the Russians had in the past. They found an apartment for her on the top of the office building where the German petroleum authorities had their Lwów headquarters. Her boss was trying to secure documents to prove that Sonia wasn't really Jewish, but only raised as a Jew. They claimed that her German-sounding maiden name, Treiner, indicated that she was of German descent. Even with this claim, such "conversion" was an impossible task. (I know of only one Jew who was granted the title of honorary Aryan and that was posthumously: Hugo von Hofmannsthal, the Jewish librettist of many Richard Strauss operas.)

Sonia could not keep her son Julek in her professional apartment, so she sent him to her parents in Stanislawow. In May 1942, six-year-old Julek was executed with his grandparents in the Jewish cemetery of Stanislawow. The Germans had gathered all the people who didn't work – hundreds of women and children – and shot them with machine guns.

The image of this child before a machine gun was intolerable to us all. Little Juleczek, as we used to call him affectionately, had been the darling of the family. Delicate, like his father, his blond hair in a curled pompadour, he symbolized the pampered, well-bred, new generation of

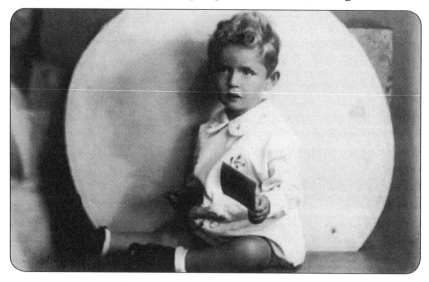

Little Juleczek, murdered in Stanislawow.

our family, its growing affluence and well-being.

My aunt and uncle were numb with grief. They must have felt guilty for not having kept the child with them, although they couldn't be blamed. It had seemed, at the time that people in smaller towns were safer. But Arthur stopped shaving and entered a period of mourning that he maintained until he was killed two years later in a concentration camp. He also stopped talking. Sonia had to continue to work and to maintain her composure while her heart was torn with grief. As the closest in age to Julek, I felt particularly vulnerable. The feeling of protection I had been afforded by the idea that I, as a child, could remain unnoticed was shattered by the bullet that killed my little cousin. Suddenly I felt that I might be next. Age no longer offered protection. Nothing did.

Julek's murder and the move to the ghetto were catalysts for our plans to escape. Ludwig was the key to our survival. We were totally dependent on his skills, talents, courage, and imagination. He had already taken the first step: he had obtained baptismal certificates for his mother and his younger sister Marysia, and escorted them on a train to the small resort town of Swoszowice, near Krakow. Even with Aryan papers, we felt it was perilous to stay in Lwów. There was a strong possibility of our being recognized by gentiles as former neighbors or acquaintances, and reported to the police. It was not uncommon for the Pole who recognized a Jew on the street to blackmail the victim; take all his money and then turn him over to the Germans. Although their hatred of the Germans was centuries old, many Poles eagerly helped in the liquidation of the Jews. These blackmailers were not motivated by greed alone; for them it was a labor of love.

Moving out of town was one way to prevent being recognized. But during the war, train traffic was very limited, and one might be forced to spend many hours at railroad stations. These became a hunting ground for professional blackmailers, who searched relentlessly for Jews with false papers. Although only people who didn't look Jewish attempted to escape in this fashion, it wasn't difficult for a Jew with Aryan looks to be recognized. The frightened look of a hunted man, the anxiety, was discernible. Many didn't make it past the railroad station. They were either apprehended or deprived of their financial resources.

After our move to the ghetto, the frequency of German raids on the Jews increased rapidly. Although it seemed that the end was swiftly approaching, we kept delaying our move to the "Aryan world." Our hesitation reflected our fear of the unknown, an inability to project ourselves into the role of Christian Poles, Catholics. Although we had known many Catholics quite well and had lived with the Nowickis for almost a year they were always seen in our eyes as strangers, goyim, those people on the other side of the fence. We felt we didn't know enough to fully identify with them, that at best we could only mimic them. Ludwig did not share our misgivings. He was busily at work forging documents, each an improvement on its predecessors. Soon our papers were ready. Two originals and one forgery. My mother had both a birth and baptismal certificate with the name Stanisłwa Heybowicz, neé Głowacka, an authentic document procured surreptitiously from the church where Ludwig's neighbor, Mrs. Heybowicz, a woman my mother's age, had been baptized. Lala's baptismal certificate read Halina Skrybayło, Mrs. Nowicka's maiden name. (Behind her back we had written to her church somewhere in Lithuania, and lo and behold three weeks later we received the real thing.) Lala was ecstatic about the name Skrybayło. She felt it conferred an air of authenticity on her baptismal certificate. Who on earth would forge a name like this? My own document was a forgery. The blank form had been bought on the black market from an "enterprising" priest. Ludwig supplied the fake stamp and we filled in the name Julian Heybowicz. Julian, because it matched my real name Julius, but sounded more Christian; Heybowicz to correspond to my mother's new last name. My new identity was complete.[2]

---

2   Sadly such practices were all too common as we fought for survival, to save our lives and the lives of our children. The forging of Christian documents and having our children such as I, assume Christian lives to save our Jewish souls became a means of survival. Even when pious Jews questioned our Rabbis if such acts were permissible, they concurred to save our lives.

Here is such an example, excerpted from the Responsa of R. Ephraim Ashri titled Emek HaBacha – The Valley of Tears. Responsa #5:

While in the Kovna Ghetto, during the days of destruction and terror against our precious children, infants and toddlers on the third and fourth day of the Hebrew month of Nissan, 5704 (1943), I was told about loving parents who, wishing to save the lives of their innocent children, purchased false documents such as birth certificates from the non-Jews and left their children in non-Jewish orphanages. Sometimes they also left their precious children in the hands of priests, who in turn wrote papers as if the children had been baptized into their faith.

Is such a thing permissible to do? I was asked. I answered that it is

Our decision to escape was made within the space of a few hours. One morning we were awakened at dawn by a cousin who lived in our new neighborhood in the ghetto. He had heard from a friend that the Gestapo was planning a major "action" for the next few days. More than four-fifths of the remaining Jews were to be taken, this time to extermination camps.

Luckily, Ludwig was in town. He had just returned from Krakow, where his mother was now living. By nine o'clock we had decided on a plan. Lala was to take the train to Krakow with Ludwig at eight that evening. My mother would go into hiding in a cellar that had a well-camouflaged door. She and ten other Jews were to stay there until the "action" was over. I was to hide in Sonia's midtown office building. Sonia would claim I was her son Julek.

We kissed each other goodbye, holding back our tears. The hope of survival was slim, that of reunion almost nil. Ludwig, himself in mortal danger, planned to return in a week and take us to Krakow one at a time. We couldn't travel together, since four Jews in a group would greatly increase the danger of discovery. My mother was afraid to travel on her own into the unknown, and I couldn't travel alone because of my age. Although it seemed to me that I had lived through decades of unrelenting terror, I was still only twelve.

Alone and numb with fear, I walked through the streets to Sonia's apartment. By then, we were not allowed to leave the ghetto without special permits, so I took off my Star of David. It was a warm, pleasant day. The central park I had to cross to reach my goal seemed more beautiful than ever. It was the first time I had entered it since

---

permissible, since doing so may save their lives. Surely if they did not hand over their children to these gentiles, they would forfeit their lives since the Nazis would murder them, heaven forbid!

If they hand over their children then they will live, and perhaps the parents themselves will survive the war and be reunited with their children and bring them back to live once again as Jews. It is also possible that those gentiles will have mercy and reveal their true Jewish identity to these children after the war, or that they will hand them over to the care of Jewish organizations. There are many possibilities that they will somehow remain Jews in order to allow this.

May the good and all merciful G-d have mercy upon us, the remnant of Israel and end our suffering, and may we see the comforting of Zion and Jerusalem.

the Germans had come, and I was surprised to discover they were maintaining it in its prewar splendor. Rows and rows of tulips of all colors grew side by side with hyacinths carefully arranged in geometric designs. Lilac trees were in full bloom. Their delicate scent reminded me of Lala's birthday, which had always been celebrated in the last week of May. Not only her room, but the whole apartment was always filled with the lilacs.

My heart was pounding. I wanted to run, but I knew it could be suicidal; they would easily spot a running Jew. I decided to skip, moving rapidly yet merging with the many children happily playing in the park. This was the first of many on-the-spot role changes I would make when faced with imminent danger. I was developing the skills of a chameleon, and it felt better, safer. I added whistling to my skipping, and the image was complete.

Unnoticed, I climbed the back staircase to Sonia's apartment. Only two other families lived on her floor, a converted attic: those of the janitor and the maintenance man, both Poles. Sonia and Arthur occupied an eight by ten foot room without a kitchen. The bathroom was in the hallway. Arthur was at home. Although I had arrived unexpectedly, he showed little surprise. No questions were asked; nothing mattered to him. I sat down in a corner and we waited in silence for Sonia's return from work.

It was dusk when she arrived. She was happy to see me. She had heard that the Germans, having uncovered many secret hiding places, had taken hundreds of Jews that day. I listened attentively, expecting her to tell me that my mother had been caught. Naturally, she didn't know. I silently wondered whether she and Arthur would adopt me if my mother was killed. We were unprotected, the only Jews outside the ghetto, trapped on top of a tall office building and anticipating a catastrophe. Sonia was very optimistic. She said that we were as safe as we could be, no one knew of our existence here.

It took me hours to fall asleep that night. I kept thinking of my father, Lala, of my mother. Sonia and Arthur were tossing and turning on their narrow bed. At one point Sonia got up to get some water.

We were awakened suddenly by a loud knocking on the door. I heard German voices. This was it! Arthur opened the door, and four fully armed German soldiers wearing helmets entered the room. They were followed by the janitor and the maintenance man with their families. It was clear who had let the Germans in. Sonia's explanations, documents, and pleadings were useless: no one was exempt. She and Arthur were to go to the Janowska camp, the gathering place for all apprehended Jews. To my surprise, the Germans didn't notice me at all. While Sonia was showing them documents, I had moved quietly to the side of the janitor's children and remained there until the Germans walked out with my aunt and uncle. The neighbors didn't notice me either. They had been unaware of my presence in the apartment. My heart was racing. I sneaked into the bathroom in the hallway and stayed there until everyone had gone to sleep. Then I returned to the room bewildered, not knowing what to do. I crawled into the warm bed and started to cry. At about nine the next morning I was awakened by voices behind the door. These were not Germans. The key turned in the lock, and to my surprise and disbelief Sonia and Arthur entered the room. They looked dreadful, but that didn't matter. At the Janowska camp Sonia had managed to convince one of the Gestapo men that her work was essential to the German war effort. He had contacted her boss, who had arranged for their release. No doubt another all-time first!

They were surprised and happy to see me. They had not known what had happened to me during their arrest. We had been saved this time, but were acutely aware that we might not be so lucky if this happened again. I was particularly endangered because I was not their child, and now the Germans knew of our existence. Sonia went to work, and Arthur and I tried to concoct a plan for my escape. Even if my mother was still alive, I could not get to her hiding place; I didn't even know where it was. Ludwig was out of town. There was no answer to my problem.

Sonia returned from work with good news. A secretary in her office, Mrs. Zagajska, was willing to take me into her suburban home for the duration of the "action." She wanted five hundred dollars or its equivalent in gold or diamonds. We had no money. Arthur suggested that we tell the woman my mother had the money and would pay her as soon as she could leave her hiding place.

At dusk, that being the safest time, I left with Mrs. Zagajska. We took the tramway and then walked a short distance. She was friendly but matter-of-fact, businesslike. I was given a tiny room in her house and warned to be very, very quiet. The warning was superfluous. I was speechless and almost paralyzed with fear. The room was quite nice, with a large iron bed, a narrow table, a chair, and cheerful flowered curtains on a small window overlooking a vegetable garden. I was given a chamber pot which was to be emptied once a day.

The Zagajskas treated me well, but I was too depressed, too bewildered to appreciate it. The food was good, but I couldn't eat. They were sorry for me. What had started as a business proposition was turning into a personal relationship. Mrs. Zagajska was my mother's age. The sight of a twelve-year-old boy gripped by fear and depression seemed to be more than she could take. She offered to accept a smaller amount of money, with the promise that after the war we would pay her double what we owed her. After I had spent a few days in total isolation she started to come in and talk with me. She had heard from Sonia that my mother was alive and on her way to Krakow. This news lifted my spirits. I knew I was to be the next taken out of Lwów by Ludwig. I could eat again.

On my tenth day of hiding, Ludwig arrived at the Zagajskas. He was full of good news. Lala and my mother were in a hotel in Krakow, waiting for my arrival. In two days we would be on our way, taking the night train. Ludwig still had some work to do on my new documents, which were to be different from the ones I had had before. They would state that I was Volksdeutsche, a Pole of German descent. Ludwig had similar papers for himself. With these documents, he explained, we could travel in the section of the train reserved for Germans. This was an important safety device against blackmailers and police informers. He had to use the new strategy because I, being male, was more vulnerable than my mother and Lala. In Poland only the Jews were circumcised. Although I didn't look strikingly Jewish, I did not look as Aryan as Ludwig did. We had to be careful.

The next two nights I did not sleep. I had serious doubts about my ability to pass for a gentile. Ludwig's plans for the new documents weren't necessarily reassuring. To me they meant that I looked Jewish and had no chance to make it on the "other side." I kept looking in the mirror. My nose was too long. My hair was brown, while most Poles were blond. My skin was fair. This was on the plus side. I tried to smile, to look cheerful, but my sad brown eyes betrayed me.

Ludwig arrived as he had promised. At dusk we left the house. Mrs. Zagajska said goodbye with tears in her eyes. She never asked for the money. Through the windows of the tramway I looked at the city of my childhood, the city of both pleasant and painful memories. It was the only city I knew. I had no time or inclination to be sentimental, but I couldn't escape the pain of saying goodbye.

The railroad station was filled with German soldiers and officers. Gigantic banners across the platform were covered with Nazi slogans. At that time Lwów was a major stopover station for the Russian front. Trying to look happy and casual, I followed Ludwig to the front to the train, the section reserved for Germans. We entered a compartment full of loud German soldiers. I was petrified. I understood a little German – my parents had spoken it between themselves when they didn't want the children to understand – but I could hardly converse in it. Ludwig, however, was unperturbed. He asked, in excellent German, whether the two seats were vacant. Minutes later we were sitting in the compartment, reading the German newspapers he had brought. I was perspiring fiercely. The print looked blurred. I wouldn't have been able to read it even if I could read German. With typical German punctuality, the train pulled away at 9:00 on the dot. I was beginning a life with a new identity.

3

The Aryan Image

The train trip was uneventful. Ludwig talked at length with the German officers in our compartment. One of them asked him why I was so pale and didn't smile. He explained to the officer that I was his cousin, recovering from a very serious case of TB. The officer wished me a speedy recovery and offered me candy. I thanked him with a silent nod of my head. Ludwig explained that I was too weak to talk.

After arriving in Krakow, we went directly to my mother's hotel. Even now, so many years later, I can't find words to describe my feelings upon seeing her and Lala in the tiny hotel room. We looked at each other in disbelief. None of us had expected that this moment would ever happen, that we would see each other again. No words were exchanged. We embraced and kissed each other in silence, tears running down our cheeks. It was the embrace relatives give one another at funerals. Death was omnipresent, and we were just being given a short respite before our next encounter with the murderers.

Our admiration for Ludwig was boundless. His behavior, especially his trip to bring me to Krakow, was heroic. He accepted our thanks matter-of-factly and with his typical modesty. He was already planning his next trip back to Lwów to save other people. The next was to be his last. It was becoming increasingly dangerous to be in Lwów: he felt that some people at work were beginning to suspect that he was Jewish. But he had to go back because he had promised to supply a friend who was in hiding with false documents.

Mother and Lala were very concerned about my looks. I was too pale. It was the height of the summer, and everyone around us was tanned. They didn't like my hair, which they said was too dark. Lala wanted me to smile more. Ludwig thought my posture wasn't right; I should walk with my chin up. I knew I was in trouble. They didn't think I looked Aryan.

Lala decided that I should have my hair bleached blond. Although shocked by this idea, I eagerly went along, thinking it would make me look more Aryan. We bought a giant bottle of peroxide and applied it to my hair. It was either our lack of expertise or some inborn resistance, but after two days of effort I became red-haired rather than blond. We panicked. Red hair is very uncommon in Poland and is associated with being Jewish. At Ludwig's suggestion we bought another bottle of peroxide. To our amazement, that did the trick: I was blond. Still I was not the image of the Polish boy we all had in mind, and we continued desperately working on my appearance. Nothing could be done about the color of my eyes or their sad expression. There were no plastic surgeons available to improve the curvature of my nose.

The only area left for possible modification was my circumcision. Ludwig learned from a dentist friend of his that a substance called Mastisol was being used in dentistry for temporary alignment of shallow incisions to make the skin stick without sutures. Ludwig's idea was to use Mastisol to mask circumcision by gluing the foreskin to the glans of the penis to make it resemble the uncircumcised specimen. Ludwig bought a bottle of Mastisol and the two of us started to experiment. I realized after the first trial that my mohel may have been a pious Jew, but he was a lousy surgeon. He hadn't left enough foreskin, and the cut wasn't even. No amount of Mastisol would cover up the mohel's mistake. Having been less than fully successful with attempts to "remake" me, we decided that if it was at all possible I would avoid going out on the street and would stay at home wherever we were going to be.

At this point we were perplexed as to where to go and what to do next. Ludwig suggested a small spa near Krakow, where we could probably rent a cheap room in a guest house; it was already off season. His mother and sister Marysia were there, and it might be easier for all of us to be in one place. The following week we rented two tiny rooms in Swoszowice, one for me and my mother and the other for Lala, who had to have a separate room as she was living under a different name from ours. We were the only tenants in the small guest house. The owner, a Polish policeman, lived with his family on the ground floor of the wooden structure; our rooms were on the second floor. There were six rooms on our floor – all empty – and one toilet. Ludwig's family was staying nearby in similar accommodations. Our room was six feet by ten feet and was furnished with one bed, a table and chair, a washbasin, and a little iron coal stove for heat and cooking. The room had a view of another small hotel, a view that was to be my only contact with the outside world in the months to come. We had almost no money left, but Ludwig managed to transfer two giant wicker baskets with clothes and linens from our apartment in Lwów.

It was a lovely sunny autumn, and for the first time in many years there was a semblance of peace and tranquility around us. Mother explained to our landlady, the policeman's wife, that she and her niece Halina (for the rest of the war, this was how she described her relationship to Lala because of the difference in our names) suffered from severe arthritis and planned to spend the winter taking the sulphur baths for which Swoszowice was famous. She didn't mention me, hoping I would remain unnoticed. We continued to obtain food by exchanging our belongings for whatever the local peasants were willing to offer. Our life centered around news from the Russian front. The Germans were having their first difficulties, and this news kept our spirits up. They were stopped in their march across Russia, and we interpreted this as the beginning of their ultimate defeat. But there would be a long wait before that happened.

Ludwig was captured and killed by the Gestapo at the end of September 1942. He went to Lwów and never returned. A week after his departure, Zosia, his mother still hadn't gotten a letter from him. We started to fear that something bad had happened. We had a very precise system of communication worked out, as there were no telephones. Ludwig was expected to mail a letter immediately upon his arrival at Lwów. He had set up a code system: Each of us had an identical sheet of paper with spaces the size of individual words. In order to write a letter, we would place the sheet on a blank piece of paper, write the message in the empty slots, remove the sheet, and fill in the rest of the space around the key words so as to make deceptively meaningful sentences. Upon receiving a letter one placed the template on top of it and read the message.

But no letter came from Ludwig. Several weeks later we learned that he had been arrested upon his arrival in Lwów – the result of a Polish informer's report to the police. He was executed a few days later.

I think I was more pained by Ludwig's death than by my father's. I had grown a great deal in the intervening year and a half. Now I clearly understood the significance of my loss. Years later, as an adult, I was to name my firstborn son Ludwig. Lala named her son after our father.

With Ludwig gone, we all felt bereaved, orphaned. Zosia seemed incapable of grasping the nature of the tragedy. After her husband had been taken away a year before, like my father, on Petliura Day, she had grown totally dependent on her son.

Lala soon took over. We were now five people, closely interdependent, a very peculiar outfit – four women and one twelve-year-old boy. Lala decided that she and Marysia, Ludwig's fifteen-year-old sister, would look for jobs as maids. I was very surprised by this decision because I remembered how much Lala had resented doing any work at home. Things must really be bad for Lala to be so willing to work, I thought. As for Marysia, I found her sweet and lovely, but I had little respect for her intelligence or common sense. The two of them got jobs working for two German families in a nearby town, while I stayed with Mother in our little room. I don't remember why my mother did not also consider working. I suppose she felt weak or depressed.

Although we spent long days together, we did not talk much until the evening, when Lala came back home from work. We had stopped talking about Father as if by mutual agreement, in order not to stir up painful feelings we could not handle. There was no talk about the dangers to our existence, about Ludwig's death, or any fears we might be experiencing. I had the impression that we all shared a feeling that there was nothing new to be said and that sharing, verbalizing our fears would only add an additional burden to an already unbearable situation. The days seemed endless, with nothing to break the self-imposed silence. I imagined that this must be how one felt in jail carrying a life sentence. I seemed to have been sentenced to this kind of penal existence merely for being a Jew; I had to wait patiently for a possible pardon.

I spent my days standing behind the curtain at the window, looking at what little action took place on the street. There was a window across from mine in the neighboring hotel, but nothing happened there either. Swoszowice, not a very exciting place even in the height of the season, was now almost deserted. One person visited us every week: a local peasant's wife, who would bring a few pounds of potatoes, and some milk in exchange for some clothes my mother gave her. By that time, our supply of clothing and linens was running low; we weighed each transaction very carefully. The peasant's family were themselves very poor. They had only a few acres of land and one cow. The wife liked to touch the fabrics of our clothes; she said she had never seen anything of such quality. In my loneliness, I tried to prolong her visits by asking questions about her cow or the last year's crops. The woman must have wondered what was going on. She, no doubt, had never had such an attentive audience.

I saw Zosia and Marysia infrequently because, as a rule we did not want the people in the village to know we knew each other well. We wanted to be sure that, if something happened to one of us, the rest would survive. Mother would meet them casually, in a store or on a bench in the park, and discuss what was happening.

Marysia lasted only two days at her job. She was fired after telling her employer she didn't know how to boil water. I guess I was right about her intelligence. We decided that it would be safer for Zosia and Marysia to move to another town in case the Gestapo had found their address on Ludwig and wanted to get them also. It was difficult to part. We were frightened by our growing isolation amid seemingly neutral but potentially hostile and dangerous strangers.

The winter of 1943 was long and painful. We had little heat. The windows were covered with frost early in December and stayed that way until March. I was cut off from the little contact I had had with the outside world. Lala was the only one to go out, leaving for her job in the darkness of the early morning hours and returning late at night. Often she would bring scraps of food from her German employers, and these would be our meal of the day. Although she worked hard, I envied her freedom and the experiences, meager though they were. In order to save on coal, we would go to bed soon after Lala got home and cover ourselves with all our blankets. My mother would read aloud the German newspaper Lala had stolen from her employer, analyzing the news from the Russian front. It seemed to us that the situation was starting to turn around. There was a flicker of hope. The Germans were caught in Stalingrad, and although it was difficult to get the true picture from the Nazi propaganda, we could read between the lines: the great victory march toward Moscow had been stopped. We understood that statements like "the German Army consolidated its defense lines" meant that they had been forced to withdraw to previous defense positions because of growing Russian pressure. It would take another two and a half years – thirty long months – until we were liberated, but to us this news meant freedom. We were ready to celebrate.

I don't know whether we would have emotionally survived that long winter but for an unexpected development. Another family moved into a room on our floor: the Kowalskis, a young Polish couple with a two-year-old boy. Mr. Kowalski was a sickly but tall and handsome man, and engineer. He suffered from tuberculosis of the spine and his doctor had recommended that he take thermal baths in Swoszowice's spa. His wife Kasia was petite with blond hair and dreamy blue eyes. She was outgoing and friendly. Before we knew it, she was spending her days in our tiny room telling my mother all her problems. This was a welcome relief from the long silent days alone, and a break in an almost nightmarish existence.

Kasia was a slightly more sophisticated version of Mrs. Nowicki, our pregnant tenant in Lwów. She was surprised to find that I lived there, having been told by our landlord, the policeman that the rooms on our floor were rented to two women. This was good news; it meant that downstairs they did not know of my existence. Still, because of my circumcision, I continued to be the most vulnerable member of our trio. To improve on their Aryan image, Mother and Lala spent hours memorizing the catechism and all the Catholic prayers commonly used in the church. It was important to know the prayers, as the Gestapo used them as a test when they suspected someone of being Jewish. It was both painful and amusing to see my mother, the proud descendent of endless generations of rabbis, reciting Hail Marys and Paternosters. Sometimes Lala became angry at her for saying the prayers without sufficient conviction. Mother would burst out crying, saying she was giving up. "I can't take it anymore!" she would scream. By then, she was very depressed and unwilling to fight for survival. She had lost the confidence she had displayed immediately after my father's capture and was now merely following directions from Lala. I was sorry for her, but Lala, feeling that the responsibility lay on her shoulders, was relentless. A few moments after crying, my poor mother was again stumbling over Hail Marys, this time being coached by Lala, to look at the picture of Christ hanging on the wall of our room and pray with determination. I was exempted from memorizing the prayers, as all that the Germans needed to do was pull down my pants to find out I was a Jew.

There was no doubt in my mind that Lala was in charge now. Although her appearance was a little too dark in this purely Slavic environment, she was mobile, determined, efficient, and knowledgeable. I was envious of her freedom of movement, and had to struggle to comprehend what was going on. In those days of war and fighting it was definitely a man's world, and to see my sister so active, so full of plans and ideas, while I was lying powerless on the bed we all shared was an overwhelming experience. I felt angry, humiliated and ashamed.

In early February, I became very ill, with severe stomach pains and a temperature close to 104 degrees for several days. We were alarmed, but we didn't know what to do. It was dangerous to call a doctor, as he would immediately see that I was circumcised. Because of the high fever I was barely conscious, but I could see my mother and Lala crying helplessly in silence, knowing, I suppose, that *I* wouldn't survive without the doctor, and that *we* would not survive with him. We could not rely on the faint hope that he would not report us to the police. And what if he recommended hospitalization?

On the fifth day of my illness, Lala came up with a brilliant idea. We would call a female doctor and I, feigning modesty, wouldn't take off my underpants. At this point I was almost delirious, but I forced myself to go over Lala's instructions on how to behave during the visit. No doctor was ever awaited with more ambivalence. I myself was amazed at how well I acted with the high fever. I screamed murder when she, suspecting appendicitis, wanted to examine the lower abdomen. I heard my mother feigning embarrassment. Deterred by my persistence, the doctor simply prescribed some medicine. A few days later I was well again.

Kasia's husband Stasiek (we were now on a first-name basis) became a frequent visitor to our little room. I watched him with curiosity.

In a letter, Zosia reported that she had gotten a job in a cigarette factory in nearby Mogila, thirteen miles from Swoszowice. (We were corresponding by means of Ludwig's pre-cut code sheets.) She also wrote that her cousin Rudolph, the photographer who had helped Ludwig prepare false papers had escaped to Krakow and that if we needed anything we should visit him. We were happy about this and felt somewhat less isolated for the first time since Ludwig's death. We decided that Lala would go to Krakow, a half-hour train ride away, on her first day off. When the day came, we were very excited. She was to discuss our plans for the future with Rudolph. We thought it advisable to leave Swoszowice in the spring and move to a bigger town, perhaps even a city, where our presence would be less conspicuous.

The days were short. Lala left early in the morning and was to return in the afternoon on the four o'clock train. Five o'clock, five thirty, six o'clock – Lala wasn't back. Mother was in frenzy, racing back and forth between our apartment and the railroad station. At six o'clock she made an announcement: Lala wouldn't be back. Mother had had a premonition that something would happen to her. "I should never have let her go," she said. "It was my fault for leaving all the responsibilities to Lala."

I looked at her in disbelief, frightened and bewildered. Why, now that Lala was gone, did Mother want to abandon me also? She knew all too well that I wouldn't have the slightest chance of making it on my own. Tears were rolling down my cheeks as my mother, now calm and composed, handed me our valuables, the little money we had, and Zosia's address. I remained silent, aggrieved. Then the door opened and Lala came in.

Before we could say a word, Lala burst out sobbing. Crying like a baby, I ran to embrace her. After she calmed down, she told us what happened. She had never gotten to see Rudolph. Upon her arrival in Krakow she had found that this was the last day of the liquidation of the Krakow ghetto. The city was full of Gestapo and German soldiers. Not knowing her way around, she had accidentally ended up near the ghetto and, after the streets were closed off, had been forced to watch the Germans round up and kill the remaining Jews. She saw a German swing a Jewish baby by the leg and smash its head against

Jews under SS guard march through Krakow during the final liquidation of the ghetto.

the wall of the ghetto, splattering its brains on the stone. I covered my ears. This was too much to take after what had just happened with my mother. I cried myself to sleep.

The next time Lala went to visit Rudolph, my mother accompanied her. I was left alone. This trip turned out even worse than the first one. They were both arrested by the Gestapo. At the railroad station in Krakow, my mother had spotted a Polish woman she knew from Lwów. Suspecting she might be an informer, Mother turned around and tried to go in the other direction, but it was too late. The woman noticed them, ran to my mother, and grabbed her by the arm. "So you are here, Mrs. Grünfeld!" she cried triumphantly. "Hiding in Krakow, no doubt, and all your diamonds safely hidden, hah?" The woman had dealt with our cousin Sidia, the musicologist, during Sidia's short career as a black-market diamond dealer, and she must have assumed that my mother was very wealthy. "It's the Gestapo or all your money," she continued.

Mother did not protest. She and Lala followed the woman to a nearby apartment house and there in the hallway gave her all their money, and their watches. The woman checked their bags, and having assured herself that she had all their possessions, walked away. It took my mother and Lala a few minutes to regain their composure and continue with their plans to visit Rudolph. When they emerged from the building, they were arrested by a member of the Polish police force, who was collaborating with the Nazis. They noticed the blackmailer grinning with satisfaction in the distance. The policeman took them directly to the Gestapo headquarters. I guess after splitting the booty with the woman he still wanted personal credit for catching two Jews, an honor that might have eluded him if he had merely escorted them to the local police precinct.

At the headquarters, Mother and Lala were asked to show their documents. These were impeccable. My mother's baptismal certificate was authentic; it read Stanislawa Heybowicz, nee Glowacka. It was accompanied by a Kennkarte, all up-to-date. Lala's documents looked equally genuine, and her last name, Skrybayło, dispelled any suspicion. Both Mother and Lala seemed very composed. Mother's depressed mood could easily have been taken for a nonchalant attitude. The Gestapo man asked my mother if she knew how to pray. Indignantly, Mother answered, "What do you mean asking whether I know how to pray? Can't you see I'm a pious woman?"

Convinced, he did not pursue the inquiry. She was lucky because, as she admitted to us later, at that moment she couldn't have recalled even one prayer. According to Lala, the Nazis did not know what to do with them next. They were obliged to pursue a full investigation once someone had been brought in under the suspicion of being a Jew, but they must have sensed that in this case, the accusation would be difficult to prove. They handed Mother and Lala their papers and let them go.

When Mother told me what happened in Krakow, I was utterly astonished. I could only think how close they had come to being killed, and how I would have never known what had happened to them. There was some encouragement in the fact that the enemy had been outwitted. Interestingly enough, I wasn't scared. I was becoming immune to those continuous threats to our lives. I was beginning to see our situation, not only as a question of individual survival, but also as a way of fighting the Germans, proving to Hitler that he was fallible. By not being able to catch me, Hitler seemed to be displaying a weakness that would eventually be his undoing. Each day of survival seemed a major victory over a truly evil force. It felt good.

I was getting genuinely annoyed and frustrated about being cooped up in our tiny room. Hearing the policeman's children playing and horsing around made me very envious of their freedom. We were slowly getting over our depression after Ludwig's death. Now we talked at length about him. He was rapidly becoming my idol, and I secretly wished to be like him when I grew up. Deprived of physical activities, I found his intellectual pursuits, his interest in art, and his self-effacing altruism particularly suitable to identify with and imitate. There was a suave sophistication about Ludwig, like that of Leslie Howard as the Scarlet Pimpernel – an ideal hero for someone in captivity. It was all mind over matter – I didn't have to throw balls or compete in sports to prove that I could be like my ideal. Daydreaming was enough.

By mid-March the frost had thawed off the windows, and I could return to the tiny slice of the world visible from my observation post behind the curtain. The pond was still frozen, and the children were having a wonderful time skating, both with and without skates. There was little traffic on the road – only a horse-drawn cart or two during a whole hour – but I wasn't bored. It was such a pleasant change from the dreary winter weather that, little as it was, it felt plentiful.

I hoped it was much colder in Russia. It was obvious by now that the Germans had suffered a serious defeat at the hands of the Russians in Stalingrad, and frost was their worst enemy. Like the French army in Napoleon's Russian campaign, the Germans could not combat the Soviets' most powerful ally – their long and merciless winter. Rudolph, whom Lala finally visited in Krakow, told her that he had seen a German train, maybe thirty cars long, full of amputees – German soldiers who had lost their limbs through frostbite in Russia – being transported back home. This was good news. Better yet, Rudolph had heard rumors that the Germans were killing off their own amputees so they wouldn't demoralize the people back home.

I was initially surprised at my reaction. Was I rejoicing to hear that hundreds of young men had lost their limbs? Yes, I was. This was not time to feign softness or compassion. Despite my tender years, I had to be brutally honest with myself; this was an all-out fight, and each dead German meant one enemy less. Although we never examined it openly in those terms, Mother and Lala must have shared my feelings, albeit with greater ambivalence. I could see this in their reaction to the new pastime I initiated. After dinner, Mother would read aloud, translating the news in the German newspaper, often from the official organ of the

Nazi party, Der Völkischer Beobachter. After she finished, I would take the last page and read aloud the obituaries. I took genuine, even sadistic pleasure in this. It seemed that either all Germans were heroic, or the greatest heroes were being killed off en masse. Page after page of announcements framed in black proclaimed the deaths on the Russian front of dozens of Ritterkreutztrager, recipients of the German Medal of Honor. They were always mourned by long lists of bereaved friends and relatives: mother, father, and best of all, a wife with a child. So I wasn't the only orphan boy. (I knew deep down that Father was gone forever. The word "dead" was difficult to contemplate; seemingly there was a distinction between the two concepts, "dead" and "gone." "Gone" felt better and I chose to use this term. But I knew he would never be back.)

We started to rate the obituaries by the number of relatives left behind. The winners were those announcements describing the dead hero as "our third son to have given his life for Führer und Vaterland." It was a sick game, but I didn't care.

Those short moments of relaxation were important; a new crisis was brewing. We were increasingly concerned with my hair. It had been a serious mistake to bleach it when I arrived from Lwów. It required continuous touch-ups which made it impossible for me to go to a barber to have my hair cut. The styles of those days were such that one needed clippers for the proper cut; scissors alone wouldn't do. Mother tried scissors, but the cut made me look so ridiculous that we decided I had to go to a barber. This turned out to be a major life-threatening proposition. How would I explain the dark roots of my blond hair to him? What would the other customers say when they saw my hair in two colors? We decided that I would try to be the first customer of the morning in order to keep the number of potential observers to a minimum. I would tell the barber that I had a strange condition; my hair had suddenly begun to change colors. I would ask him for advice about what to do.

We were all very tense the evening before I was to go to the barber. None of us slept. I got up at dawn in order to leave the house before the policeman and his family were up and waited at the entrance of a church near the barber shop for several hours, shivering from cold. At nine, Mother and Lala arrived. They were to watch from a distance in case emergency intervention was needed. To my amazement, when I entered the shop, I was calm and composed. The barber, a stocky man in his forties, was pleased to see an early customer. Heat was radiating from an almost glowing iron stove. He looked puzzled and, I think, suspicious when I told him my story. He had never heard of a change of color such as I described. He was reluctant to cut, and suggested I see a doctor first. I told him that I couldn't stay like this as other children were making fun of me, and I requested a crew cut to get rid of all my blond hair. Reluctantly, he started to cut. Not having been cut properly for almost six months, my hair was long, and the switch to a crew cut was truly dramatic. Strange as I may have looked with my bleached blond hair, I was positively frightening with short brown hair. I could not contain my tears.

My ordeal was almost over when another customer entered the shop. He looked in disbelief from the blond hair on the floor to my dark head. I was afraid he would ask questions, but he didn't. I paid and left as fast as possible, covering my head with a woolen knit hat. Out of the corner of my eye I could see the barber and the customer watching me through the shop window. I was sure they knew I was a Jew.

The events that followed occurred so rapidly that we never figured out whether or not they were related to the barber incident. Early in the morning two days later, soon after Lala left for work, Mrs. Kowalski knocked on our door. I knew at once that something important had happened. She asked my mother to come to her room without delay. My mother left and, sensing danger, I started to dress rapidly. Mother was back within minutes. It turned out that the policeman's wife had met Mrs. Kowalski in the bakery that morning and had told her of rumors in the village that we were Jews hiding on false papers. She wondered whether Mrs. Kowalski, being our next-door neighbor, had also suspected this. The policeman's wife herself wasn't sure. My mother didn't look Jewish at all; the only strange thing about us was that I never went out to play with other children. Her husband was going to talk to the commander of the precinct and volunteer to investigate the situation. She would be terribly embarrassed, she said, if she was found to be hiding Jews in her house – even inadvertently. For her own sake, she hoped the rumor was false.

I was shocked to find out that they knew I lived there. How stupid we had been to believe that my existence could be hidden! Looking back, I realized that there had been countless giveaways: a doctor had seen me when I was ill, and the farmer's wife visited us weekly – how could we have imagined the policeman and his wife would not know about me? I was still a child; my naiveté was excusable, but Mother? Lala? I felt that they couldn't be depended on anymore.

By the time Mother had finished telling the story, I was dressed and ready to go. We had no time to waste. Being the "corpus delicti," I had to leave first. We decided that I would wait at the railroad station until five o'clock, when Lala came home from work. There was no way of letting her know about the latest development before then. In the meantime, my mother would pack our belongings and join us at the station. Having been released once by the Gestapo, she was more confident of her ability to convince people she wasn't a Jew. With me out of the way, she was sure she would be able to handle the police investigators, even if they came immediately. She had no choice but to pack our belongings; if we arrived at lodgings without luggage, it would be obvious that we were Jews on the run.

For me it was a long day of waiting. It seemed the afternoon would never come. The tiny railroad station was empty most of the time, and I was nervous about arousing suspicion. Around eleven in the morning I approached the station master and told him that I was waiting for my aunt, who must have missed her train. He too was bored, and he invited me into his little office, which was warm and cozy. Mother came at three o'clock and we agreed on this plan: Lala would stay in Swoszowice overnight and send our luggage to Warsaw the following morning by the railway express. Meanwhile Mother would take me to Krakow, where we would stay at Rudolph's. The following day Mother and Lala would leave for Warsaw. I would go to Zosia's and wait there until I could join them. Warsaw seemed our best bet because it was a big city. The bigger the place, the easier it should be to go unnoticed, to dissolve into the background.

Lala accepted our plan without hesitation. She didn't mind the risk of staying alone overnight in our room, agreeing that without our belongings, we had no chance of survival. It was amazing how easily we negotiated during our emergencies, and how willingly we each contemplated sacrificing our own lives for the survival of the others. It was teamwork at its most sublime, and it worked.

Rudolph was surprised to see Mother and me, but eager to help. Rudolph was tall and well built, with curly brown hair and gentle blue eyes. There was an air of sophistication about him; one could easily detect the sensitivities of an artist photographer. He was Ludwig's first cousin, and they had worked on a book together during the Soviet occupation.

Lala arrived safely the following morning. The police hadn't shown up and she had managed to ship our luggage to Warsaw, general delivery, to be picked up upon her arrival.

Mother and Lala left for Warsaw by the night train. As there were no telephones, we wrote to Zosia, who lived some thirteen miles from Krakow. We asked whether she could keep me until Lala returned to bring me to Warsaw, having found a place to stay and, we hoped, jobs. Zosia responded promptly. It would not be advisable for me to live with her, she wrote, as it might arouse suspicion, but she did have a place for me with a local peasant who was looking for lodgers in order to make some extra money. Rudolph accompanied me to the farm. I received a royal welcome there, being in all likelihood the first city person the family had ever entertained. Unfortunately, the welcome was all they had to offer.

Spring is always a difficult time for Polish peasants. They have eaten almost all their crops and slaughtered their pigs. All that remains are some potatoes that have been stored during the winter in a deep ditch covered with straw to protect them from frost. It seems hard to believe, but despite the fact that they have practiced this method of storage for generations, the peasants are apt to find in the spring at least half of their potatoes frozen and thus a barely edible, rotting, sweet-tasting mush. We were fed such potatoes twice a day, along with the sour-tasting soup called *kvass*. We ate in true peasant style: one big wooden bowl with soup, another with hot potatoes. The whole family sat around the table and a wooden spoon was passed around clockwise.

The farmer I stayed with was very poor. His only source of income was a single cow. Each day his wife walked nine and a half miles to the city carrying two large cans of milk. I felt sorry for them and wanted to help, but the soil was still frozen and there was no work. We spent the days around the giant wood-burning kitchen stove keeping warm.

I went to Zosia's after ten days, expecting Lala to come at any time to pick me up. To my surprise there had been no letter from Mother, no news at all since they had left Rudolph's. I was extremely worried, feeling helpless and left behind again. Zosia tried to reassure me, blaming the slow postal service for the lack of news, but she seemed equally worried. I didn't dare ask questions. Marysia, her daughter seemed completely oblivious to what was going on.

The few days that followed were probably, for me, the worst of the whole war. I was totally overwhelmed by the possibility that Mother and Lala had perished in Warsaw. I panicked. For the first time since the beginning of our odyssey, I turned to G-d. My parents had always acted as if they were religious; we kept a kosher home and celebrated major holidays, and I used to pray when my grandmother Zippora visited us. I had always sensed, however, that all this was mostly ceremonial, "to keep the tradition," in my father's words. G-d was rarely mentioned at home. Now in Mogila, in Zosia's home, I started to pray, silently promising G-d that I'd be a believer if He would bring Mother back to me. This was a kind of "in case" promise. In case there was a G-d, I could use His help. I could use anyone's help. Once the situation was again under control, my beliefs faded rapidly. I knew I was alone.

The days seemed endless. I spent mornings at the window, waiting for the postman. After his arrival, with no mail for us, I waited for Zosia to come back from work. She would guess from the expression in my eyes that there was no news. She no longer tried to cheer me up; she could not have helped. I ate little or nothing.

I just turned thirteen the week I was staying with Zosia. I was acutely aware that it was my birthday, but I didn't tell anyone. Although we had not celebrated our birthdays since the war broke out, this year I was making a statement: If Mother and Lala weren't alive, my birthday meant nothing. In retrospect I find it puzzling that the fact that this would have been the year of my bar mitzvah didn't even cross my mind.

Three weeks after Mother's departure, Zosia suggested that we go to Krakow on Sunday to consult Rudolph about what we should do next. I couldn't stay in Mogila much longer, as this would arouse suspicion. Where could I go? How could I live on my own at my age? In a matter of days I would be caught by the police. It was then that I realized I had reached the end. It was either suicide or waiting to be killed. Ludwig had once suggested that we carry a dose of cyanide to poison ourselves if we were caught. We never got hold of the poison. I hoped that Rudolph had some, or could obtain it for me. It would be fast and painless.

On Saturday, the day before we were to go to Krakow, a letter arrived from Lala. The postman looked at me in disbelief when I started to sob uncontrollably, pressing the letter against my chest.

Lala's letter didn't make sense at all. In my excitement I had forgotten that she was using Ludwig's sheet, and I was reading it straight. With the code sheet applied, it had good news. Mother and Lala were settling down in Warsaw. Mother was already working as a live-in maid for a German general and his wife. Lala had found a place to stay; she was renting a bed in the apartment of a Polish widow, Mrs. Krawczyk, who was willing to take me in as a boarder also. Lala was coming to pick me up in a few days. I felt relieved. I was convinced, however, that there wouldn't be a happy ending next time and remained determined to get the cyanide.

Even under those circumstances, where we were all in hiding, I seemed to be getting the raw end of the deal. Lala was out every day working, and I had to act as though I didn't exist. I tried to read but could not concentrate.

We all needed new clothes badly. Upon Mother and Lala's arrival in Warsaw, they had found that almost everything of any value had been pilfered from the two giant wicker baskets Lala had sent, risking her life, from Swoszowice.

Their trip to Warsaw had been uneventful. On the train they had met a Polish woman who had invited them to stay with her until they were settled. Mother got her job through a newspaper. She was working for General Herr Felix Feldschuh and was very unhappy. The job was strenuous, and she was continually abused by Frau Feldschuh, who called her "Polnischer schweinhund" and once slapped her in the face for breaking a glass. Mother couldn't leave that job until she found another one; she had nowhere to stay in the meantime. Lala had been fortunate: on the street she had met a friend of the past, Tadzio, who was now living in Warsaw on false papers.

I remember Tadzio very well. He had visited Lala often during the Russian occupation. He was short and blue eyed, with curly blond hair. He looked somewhat effeminate despite his well-built body. Tadzio had an encyclopedic knowledge of all world records; he was a Polish, living version of The Guinness Book of Records. For whatever reason, I was fascinated by his cornucopia of trivia and I filled my head with nonsense; Amelita Galli-Curci, the world's best singer; Jesse Owens, the fastest runner, and so forth.

In Warsaw, Tadzio found the place for Lala at Mrs. Krawczyk's. He was living nearby. Lala and I decided to leave by train for Warsaw the following evening, so as not to prolong the danger to Zosia by our presence. As always now, the focus of our concern was on my looks; I was very pale. The anxiety of the past few weeks was still discernible in my eyes, and my almost black, four-week-old crew cut complemented the picture in a very unbecoming way. The consensus was that I looked very Jewish. To my great surprise, it was Marysia who came up with an excellent idea. The neighbor's father was a former Polish army officer; she would steal his army cap for me to wear on the train. Those caps were very rare then; although they were worn without any insignia, people who had them on were seen as displaying a high degree of Polish patriotism, a demonstration of political resistance. No one would suspect a boy wearing this cap of being a Jew. To improve on the image, I suggested that I carry a large bouquet of flowers to cover my face. It is customary in Poland to give flowers as a going-away present, so people carrying flowers on the train were not an uncommon sight. With the flowers and the cap in my possession, I felt almost safe. We were getting the feel, by then of the right constellation of attributes needed to generate the Aryan image. I was looking forward to the trip, to seeing Mother and Warsaw, the famous capital.

Our trip went smoothly. I tried not to sleep, so that I could keep the giant pot of white azaleas on my lap all through the seven-hour-long trip. We had decorated the plant with red ribbons, red and white being the Polish national colors. Between the cap and the red and white flower pot I must have looked like a living monument to the defeated Polish army. That was fine with me.

An hour from Warsaw, our train stopped at a small station; I don't recall its name. To my horror I noticed, standing on the opposite track, a cargo train full of Jews. The train cars had small barred windows in the upper corners, reinforced on the outside with barbed wire. In those windows, we could see several panic-stricken faces. The prisoners were shouting something to the passengers in our train. After a while I understood the words. They asked us where were they going. Where were they being carried off to? It was clear from the anguished, terrified voices that they knew where they were headed. No one answered their questions. There was a dead silence among the eight passengers in our compartment. I didn't even dare to look at Lala for fear that one of us might burst out crying. We knew by then, through Rudolph and Mr. Kowalski, about Auschwitz, Majdanek, and Treblinka, the worst of the extermination camps. But never during the whole war had we dared to discuss or even comment on this among ourselves. It was too close, too frightening, and too real.

Our train pulled away, leaving the screaming prisoners in the agony of their helplessness. An old lady in my compartment crossed herself and then took out the rosary, her lips moving in silence. I wished that I could believe in a helping G-d.

4
Warsaw

It was a beautiful Sunday morning in April 1943 when we arrived in Warsaw. The railroad station was humming with people carrying packages of various shapes and sizes. These packages, as I found out later, contained food of all kinds being smuggled from the countryside to the capital. Lacking regular supply channels, people had to travel to villages around Warsaw to buy the food directly from the farmers. The Germans were opposed to this system and would often confiscate the produce on the train. To prevent this from happening, people wrapped the food around their bodies: slabs of bacon would take the shape of a belt; ten pounds of kasha made a woman look very pregnant.

Fascinated by the peculiar sights around me, I forgot to worry about being discovered at the station. We went directly to our place on 20 Gibalski Street. On the way Lala told me that our landlady, Mrs. Krawczyk, was a widow in her early thirties, and her son, Edek, was my age. The apartment consisted of one room and an eat-in kitchen. There was no bathroom, as the apartment house had not

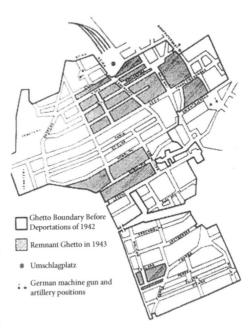

☐ Ghetto Boundary Before Deportations of 1942

▨ Remnant Ghetto in 1943

⊛ Umschlagplatz

⁑ German machine gun and artillery positions

Warsaw Ghetto

been finished when the war broke out in 1939. There were communal outhouses in the yard for the tenants of the five-story walk-up. Water had to be brought up from a well downstairs.

Mrs. Krawczyk didn't know we were related. Lala had told her that I was the son of a close friend who worked as a maid in the city. This meant that I would have to address my sister from now on with the formal "Pani Halino," the accepted form in Polish between strangers. There was one other tenant in the apartment, Mietek, Mrs. Krawczyk's twenty-five-year-old nephew.

As there were only four beds in the room, I would have to share one with Edek. Lala described Edek as a friendly but tough boy who stole things from his mother and sold them in local stores. Lala had convinced Mrs. Krawczyk to take me into their overcrowded apartment by telling her that I was a model child and would have a lasting beneficial effect on Edek's behavior.

The situation was too ridiculous to worry about. In addition to hiding the fact that I was a Jew, I had to pretend that Lala was a stranger, share a bed with a boy who was tough and sneaky, and share a room with four other people. As if this weren't enough, I had to be a model child, a positive influence on a kid I was afraid of before I even laid eyes on him!

The apartment house on Gibalski Street looked worse than I had imagined. It was nine o'clock on a Sunday morning; the first thing that struck me was the sight of three small outhouses in the center of the yard, and long lines of people in pajamas and nightgowns in front of them. There were two five-story apartment houses looking raw and unfinished, just the basic structure, beams and concrete still exposed. The staircase had no rails, and our apartment lacked a doorknob and doorbell.

Mrs. Krawczyk was very pleased to see us. I thought I noticed an expression of surprise when she laid eyes on me. Was I being self-conscious? Or wasn't I the image of the country boy she had thought would reform her reprobate son? I felt awkward and anxious. Fortunately, Edek was still asleep, so I had time to get the feel of the place. The room was quite large. There were four iron beds, one in each corner. The walls were exposed brick without plaster, unpainted. An armoire and a table with four chairs were the only other items in the room. The window which had no curtain, faced another unfinished structure.

To gain time to get adjusted and to delay meeting Edek, I asked Lala to tell Mrs. Krawczyk that I was very tired. She understood that I must be tired after the long trip and told me to go and lie down in her bed so as not to awake Edek. I was somewhat surprised at this suggestion but didn't say anything. It turned out later that our landlady was unfamiliar with the concept of personal beds; during my stay there we all changed beds quite frequently. After having shared the same spoon with six peasants in Krakow, I felt this to be a minor inconvenience.

In the afternoon we went to see my mother, who had Sunday off. Lala had arranged to meet her in the hallway of a large apartment house in the exclusive section of Warsaw, then inhabited by families of German occupation forces and their civilian administration. (Poland had by that time been formally annexed by Germany, with General Hans Frank as governor.) Mother almost didn't recognize me in my army cap. She looked exhausted; the job was too much for her. She had good news for Lala though. A relative of General Feldschuh, her boss, was opening a dental practice for German civilians in Warsaw and was looking for a receptionist. Lala could go for an interview on Monday. We spent about half an hour talking in the hallway. Fearing the cumulative effect of our Jewish looks, we were afraid to walk together on the street. We decided to meet every Sunday in the same place, since it seemed safe. Mother had brought some food she had stolen from her employer, and we took it back to Mrs. Krawczyk's house.

Edek was shy when we met. He seemed uneasy, avoiding eye contact. He was somewhat taller than I, wiry and muscular. His hair was blond, that enviable blond that all those bottles of peroxide had never delivered. Despite his physical superiority, I felt that I was the stronger one. Although I was vulnerable now, I knew that my weakness was transient, while his was permanent. He was a child born out of wedlock to a simple Polish woman and according to Lala, was naïve and of marginal intelligence. My four years of cunning brinkmanship gave me what may have been a feeling of superiority and self-confidence. We avoided each other for a while. The only problem was the sleeping arrangement. We both felt awkward sharing a bed without even knowing each other. The bed was narrow, but we managed not to touch.

The next morning Edek introduced me to his friends. We had seen them earlier on the line to the outhouse, but with everyone eagerly awaiting his turn in what seemed to me an endless wait, that was not the place to get acquainted. I tried to look casual when we met "the gang" as Edek called them, but I was petrified. I had never been the paragon of a sportsman, and now, after two years of inactivity, I knew my awkwardness and inexperience could easily be detected. Curiously enough, the boys were not interested in sports. Their main pastime was the gang war they were waging against a group of boys from a neighboring housing project. This must have been their way of identifying with the war that was raging around us; sports are a peacetime hobby.

In the lobby of our building, Rysiek, the gang leader, gave instructions. The weapons were stones, with which after lunch, we were to fill our pockets and attack our neighbors.

Fortunately, I was ignored. I didn't yet belong. I stayed home after lunch, waiting for Edek's return. He was back after a short while, saying that the neighbors ran away after seeing "our" gang descend on them with full pockets. I decided that the following Sunday, after seeing my mother, I would practice throwing stones in her neighborhood in case I was asked to join.

Lala got her job. She told me that Dr. Herbert Schmoll, her employer, practiced dentistry in an SS uniform. He must have been taken with Lala's appearance. Even before asking about her qualifications he had inquired whether she was married. He greeted his patients with "Heil Hitler!" and kept Hitler's portrait in every room of his spacious office. We had figured out by then that it was safer to work for the Germans than for the Poles. A Pole could find nuances in our behavior that were specifically Jewish, reflecting our different upbringing. It might be anything: a way of talking about a holiday, a phrase, and attitude. The Germans, on the other hand, could not discern the difference; for them all Poles were the same, members of an inferior race.

A week later Mother found a new job as a maid to one of Lala's boss's patients. Mother's new employer, Herr Heinrich Rockschmidt, was a civilian. He owned a large German trucking company, whose headquarters were now in Warsaw; his firm was supplying the German army on the eastern front. Rockschmidt's family – his wife and two children – were on their estate near Berlin; Mother would be more independent, actually in charge of the Warsaw household.

The first crisis at Mrs. Krawczyk's came a week after my arrival. It was Saturday night, time for the weekly bath in a tin tub placed for that purpose in the center of the kitchen. In order to save on hot water, Mrs. Krawczyk decided that I would take a bath together with Edek. Until then I had acted extremely shy when we were dressing or undressing, so Edek could not see my circumcision. Now came the moment of truth. There were no two ways about it; I had to take off my clothes in order to take the bath. I was procrastinating and Mrs. Krawczyk was getting impatient. I was supposed to be the model child, wasn't I? I was frantic. But moments later I had a plan. There was no electricity; the house hadn't been wired when the war broke out, and a glass petroleum lamp on the table was our sole source of light. I decided to risk my landlady's wrath and break the lamp, "accidentally," of course. Hearing the breaking glass, Mrs. Krawczyk came running into the kitchen. She was furious, suspecting Edek at first. I apologized profusely, and while she went to buy a new lamp I proceeded to undress in the total darkness and join Edek in the bathtub. I planned to make him more self-conscious in the future, so that in the following weeks we would take our baths separately.

The next Monday I was formally admitted to the gang and participated in the first stone-throwing fight. My performance was poor, to put it mildly: most of my stones fell halfway between us and the enemy. I overheard someone saying "sissy," which bothered me; I didn't want to stand out. I had been very apprehensive since my arrival in Warsaw. It was the first time since we had escaped from Lwów that I was not in hiding. Every waking minute I felt in danger of being discovered, of making a slip, the wrong move that would become my undoing. It was April of 1943, the month of the uprising in the Warsaw Ghetto and the final liquidation of Warsaw's Jewish population. When we arrived from Krakow, we saw whole sections of the ghetto in flames. The odor of burning bodies permeated the air. Occasionally, we saw small groups of Jews who had managed to get to the streets outside the ghetto, running

German soldiers watch the Warsaw Ghetto burn.

from the German and Polish police. The topic of escaping Jews and the burning ghetto was daily fare on our block. People suggested excursions to the ghetto to "watch the Yids burn." When escaping Jews were seen running through the streets, comments like "I hope they catch them soon" were usually made.

One evening a group of Jews came into our yard. There were five of them; probably a family. Two men, a woman and two teen-age boys. They were haggard and dirty. Their clothes were in shreds. They appeared as if out of nowhere, possibly from a manhole of the sewage system, and asked for directions, I don't recall to where. It was dusk. A few children were playing in the area and several adults stood nearby. No one answered their question. The fugitives looked frightened but tough; there was no one with the panic I had seen in the eyes of the people on the train to Auschwitz. They must have been fighters from the ghetto uprising. They looked determined not to give up, I thought. Rebuffed by my neighbors, they exchanged words in Yiddish among themselves. Then suddenly the oldest man in the group pulled out a gun and, pointing it at the few bystanders, commanded, "We are hungry. Give us some food, fast!"

We all watched in disbelief. I was proud but terrified. Despite their toughness they seemed very vulnerable. The Poles hesitated briefly but then walked briskly to our building followed by the group, the gun still in the man's hand.

I was apprehensive that someone would call the police while they were getting the food and wanted to warn them, but knew that to do so would be suicidal. I became very agitated, not knowing what to do. For a split second I even considered joining them, fighting the Germans openly, shooting it out with them. The thought did not last long. Two years before, at the beginning of the German occupation, I would probably have done it without hesitation. But now I was becoming cynical: it wasn't honor, it was survival that counted. The Jews left after a few minutes, slices of bread in their hands. They disappeared rapidly into the darkness of the April evening. I watched them in silence, praying in Hebrew for their survival.

The incident left our building in an uproar. It was hard to believe the virulence of the explosive discussion. Comments like "We should have strangled them ourselves" and "Those stupid Germans will let them all escape" flew across the yard. The turmoil would probably have continued for quite a while had it not been for the sudden arrival of a truckload of German police. I had been right to suspect that someone would report the Jews to the authorities. The Germans charged into the building in hot pursuit, hitting bystanders with nightsticks. I secretly smiled with satisfaction.

The month of May was relatively tranquil, without major upheavals. Fortunately for me, Rysiek, the gang leader was shot down by the Germans when he crossed the street to visit his cousin after the 8:00 p.m. curfew. The gang was disbanded, and I now played with Edek mostly at home. Lala was very pleased with her job; she was earning a decent salary *Lala at work in the* and was stealing little chips of gold from old *dental office.* fillings and pulled teeth. Dr. Schmoll was very kind to her; she became his chief assistant almost immediately.

Her boss's main interest besides dentistry was the extermination of Jews, and he would tell Lala and his patients how sorry he was that he had been assigned to a practice in Warsaw rather than a place like Auschwitz. Lala knew that this was a lie; he had chosen to stay in Warsaw when he was not allowed to take his mistress along to the concentration camp. He claimed to be able to recognize a Jew just by his odor, without even looking. He always wanted to know whether Lala, as a Pole, subscribed to his views. To her astonishment, Lala found that among the seven people working in his laboratory and office there were two other Jews with false papers. She got an inkling of this once, when during a coffee break, they tried to outdo the good doctor in their anti-Semitic remarks; their comments lacked the authenticity of a Polish anti-Semite. I found Lala's report of Jews hiding in an SS man's office truly encouraging. I was waiting for the day, after the war, when we would be able to tell him the truth.

It seemed now, in the fourth year of the war, that there was hope we would see the end of it. The Germans were being defeated on the Soviet front and were suffering losses in Italy following their debacle in Africa. We were impatient with the Allies in Italy, who were taking their time before conquering Rome, but this did not discourage us. For the first time since we had turned in our Telefunken radio to the Ukrainian police in Lwów, we were able to listen daily to the news in Polish from BBC. Herr Rockschmidt, being a German, was allowed to have a radio in his apartment, and when he went out my mother would tune in to the news. The BBC was then the hub of the European communications system, and news in all European languages was beamed round the clock into the territories occupied by the Germans. As in the times when my father was listening to the radio, each newscast was preceded by the familiar first four notes of Beethoven's Fifth, the "Fate" Symphony. These notes became the symbol of hope and freedom for all occupied Europe.

Mother was also satisfied with her job. Rockschmidt traveled extensively, so she was almost completely independent. In the boss's absence the office was managed by his uncle, a Pole (Rockschmidt had Polish blood in him) who also treated Mother well, and she was now able to supply us with almost unlimited amounts of food. She didn't tell her employer about my existence, as people in those days were reluctant to hire domestics with children, fearing that the women would steal food for them. Now in charge of the household, Mother tried to get the best possible nourishment for me. I was growing rapidly, and she feared for my health. She was especially concerned about TB, after the years of malnutrition in Lwów and Swoszowice.

With Mother and Lala more or less settled, I, as usual, was the one in a precarious situation. Although I was getting along with Edek, and Mrs. Krawczyk felt I was exerting a positive influence on him (I myself thought he had improved because there was nothing left to steal at home) it seemed to us that I was overexposed in our building, that eventually someone would suspect me of being a Jew. Lala and I were working hard on that still elusive Christian image. Grace at every meal, and prayers kneeling in front of the pictures every night, became routine. On Sundays we went to church with our landlady, her nephew Mietek, and Edek. Fortunately, Mrs. Krawczyk preferred the new national Catholic Church which had dispensed with individual confession. It would have been very difficult to bluff through one-to-one confession if we had gone to a regular church. Once a month, Mrs. Krawczyk would force us to join her on a pilgrimage to some obscure place where a new church was being dedicated. This often meant walking on our knees from one picture of a saint to another, our shins grazed and bleeding from the raw concrete floor.

Until that time I had not been aware how great a role religion played in people's lives. Although this religious fervor was no doubt intensified by the war and the need to feel protected in a time of peril, I found the constant onslaught of such demands burdensome. Soon after my arrival in Warsaw, Edek wanted to see a picture of my first Communion. Poverty notwithstanding, everyone my age in our building seemed to have an elaborate photograph of their confirmation ceremony. Despite the shortage, a black suit was de rigueur. Typically, it was embellished by a white carnation on the lapel, and a white ribbon with a bow on the left arm. I explained to Edek that I had left my picture with relatives in Krakow, but this answer did not satisfy his mother, who felt that all Christian children should have their Communion pictures hanging over their beds. Edek had his. I told her that I would write and ask to have it sent, but two weeks later, when nothing had arrived, she urged me to write again. A new crisis was brewing. Edek started to tease me, saying I never did have a Communion – an ultimate disgrace – and that was why I did not have a picture from the ceremony. A few days later all our "friends" on the block knew about the missing picture. I was becoming alarmed; I didn't want anyone to wonder whether I had had a Communion.

Typically, Lala came up with a solution. She took a photo of me to a photographer near her job and told him that this was the picture of her brother who had died of TB just a few days before his first Communion. Her brother's last wish had been to have a Communion picture; although his wish had not come true, she wanted the photographer to make a photomontage, to create a Communion picture to console her poor mother who, by the way, was a war widow. Lala had tears in her eyes telling this story, and the photographer was so moved that he offered to do the work for free.

I myself was impressed with the finished product. I looked very dignified in the dark blue suit above which he had pasted my head. He must have retouched my eyes; I recall that I was smiling in the original picture, while now my eyes looked blissful and dreamy. Not only did the picture look authentic, it was bigger and better than any of the other pictures I had seen in my building. I guess the photographer, moved by Lala's story, had wanted to enshrine me among the saints. The picture met with complete approval, and even some expressions of envy among our neighbors. My prestige in the building skyrocketed, and a sister of one of Edek's friends sent a message that she liked me.

No sooner were we over the Communion escapade than Edek had a new trick up his sleeve. Having given up stealing, his main interest now was religion. Under his tutelage all the unanswered questions that had plagued me in Swoszowice were more than clarified. However, when he suggested that we become altar boys in our local church, I was astonished. I found the idea both ridiculous and incredible. What next?

Having no privacy in the one-room apartment, I could not tell Lala what was going on, and I often had to wait a whole week, until Sunday, when I could share my problems with Mother. Lala could not contain her laughter the following day, when she returned from work to find me and Edek wearing Mrs. Krawczyk's white nightgowns, practicing our future assignment as altar boys. Edek was the priest, and I was to give him the liturgical responses. "Dominus Vobiscum," Edek intoned in a singsong voice, waving a candle. I looked somewhat lost, but he coached me willingly. "Et in spiritu tuo" was my line. Fortunately, the local church turned out to have no need for additional altar boys. I sighed with relief.

We were now convinced that the war would be over soon, and that the German defeat was only months away. The Polish resistance was very active, killing important German officers and sabotaging railroads that carried badly-needed supplies to the faltering Russian front. The Germans were impeded by these activities, which forced them to intensify their surveillance of railroads and assign more army men to protect their important military commanders. They decided on Draconian retaliatory measures to stop the sabotage activities.

Unable to capture the members of the resistance army inflicting the damage, they declared that for each assassinated German, ten Polish men from Warsaw would be publicly executed. At almost regular intervals the city was plastered with giant white posters carrying the ominous warning and signed by Governor Frank. A week later, the Germans unexpectedly surrounded one of the busiest blocks in the city, randomly picked ten men who happened to be in the area, placed them against a wall and machine-gunned them in front of the horror-stricken passersby. The still-bleeding bodies were loaded on a truck and driven away.

The following day new placards announced the names of the executed. They also listed fifty other men arrested on the street that day who were being kept as hostages to be executed at the ratio of ten to one if more German officers were assassinated by the Polish resistance.

These developments considerably aggravated the already critical situation I had found since my arrival in Warsaw. Swoszowice with its depressing monotony seemed a symbol of tranquil security by comparison. Here in Warsaw, the danger of my situation was undeniable. I felt highly vulnerable. I was running for my life, my potential captors always around the corner. It was getting more and more difficult to catch my breath.

In July, Lala found me a job as a messenger-delivery boy for another German dentist. The timing was perfect, because one of the boys in our courtyard had called me "Jew boy." I wasn't sure whether this was just a general insult or an opinion about my background, and I could not afford to wait to find out. We felt that it would be safer if I moved to another neighborhood and didn't push my luck. My new job was particularly suitable because the dentist, Dr. Renate Brabetz, was a former associate of Dr. Schmoll, Lala's boss, and had a dental lab with a room for me to sleep in. I could start working in a week, and I hoped that nothing would happen before then in the apartment on Gibalski Street.

I was looking forward to living alone, protected from the constant minor crises that now impinged on my privacy. I was exhausted by being "on stage" all day long. Even just talking was trying; with our different assumed surnames I had to act as if Lala was a stranger. Amazingly, I had never made a slip and called her Lala. It was always the formal "Pani Halino." Never a mistake, never a minute to relax the vigil. I knew I wouldn't miss Edek; we had always been worlds apart even though, as time passed, he started to copy many of my habits. He had lost his father in combat at the beginning of the war in 1939, two years before I had lost mine; like me, he must have been searching for someone to identify with. Although it was to my advantage, I felt a little guilty when he became genuinely modest, undressing behind a screen, while my shyness was just a sham. I had also become fond of Mrs. Krawczyk. She was kind and giving, sharing with us the little food she could obtain in those days. I might consider her a mother substitute if only she hadn't been such a devout Catholic. One of her great virtues was her cleanliness, an almost Sisyphean task under our circumstances.

Besides not having a bathroom and running water, we were plagued by hordes of bedbugs that nestled comfortably in the cracks of our plaster less walls. Night is the bedbug's prime time, probably an evolutionary development based on availability of prey. To put it in simpler terms, it was impossible to sleep in Mrs. Krawczyk's apartment. At two a.m., when dozens of merciless bugs were out in force, our landlady would wake us up and we would start our counterattack. DDT had not yet been discovered, at least we didn't know about it in Poland, and its predecessors were ineffective. The work had to be done manually: grab a bedbug and squeeze the life out of it. I preferred bedbugs to lice: the former made their homes in the walls, while the latter nestled on one's body or in one's hair. Bedbugs being Mrs. Krawczyk's domain, Lala became an expert on head lice. After our Saturday bath, now taken individually in the darkened kitchen, she would comb our hair with a special fine-toothed comb and search for the remaining nits. The simple chores of wartime existence!

We told Mrs. Krawczyk that I was going back to Krakow. A week later Lala introduced me to my employer, Dr. Brabetz. I went for the interview carrying my suitcase, as Lala had told her that I was the child of an acquaintance, a domestic: not being able to live with my mother, I needed a place to sleep as well as a job. I felt awkward and very nervous, to say the least. Lala told me that Dr. Brabetz didn't really need a messenger boy, but that she herself, having me in mind for the job, had sold her the idea when the dentist was still an associate of Dr. Schmoll. My responsibilities were poorly defined.

Many things had happened in the thirteen years of my life, but nothing had really prepared me for a job interview. My concerns were basic: I wondered whether I would be able to keep a job like this. My life depended on it, as I had nowhere to go should the dentist fire me. Also, my future employer would be the first German I had talked to directly, and this added greatly to my apprehension. Dr. Brabetz spoke only German; my German was rudimentary.

We took the tram to the fashionable downtown area of Warsaw and then walked several blocks to the new, exclusively German neighborhood, the most elegant in the city. We walked very slowly. I held Lala's hand tightly and tried to make the short walk as long as possible. We were both silent, preoccupied with our thoughts. Mine were a mixture of fear and rage. I felt I did not deserve this constant onslaught of painful experiences. The neighborhood, with German children happily playing and skipping around me, underlined my feeling of personal injustice. In the Polish section of Warsaw everyone was more or less a victim of war. Food was scarce, spaces crowded, and passersby looked haggard and sad, besides being undernourished. Here, in the German section, one would never have guessed that this was the fourth year of a raging world war. I wished a bomb would explode on the lovely street and tear the playing children to pieces. All of them!

Suddenly, the happy prattle around me seemed to stop. I heard a deafening explosion followed by ear-piercing screams. Everything around me looked red, bloody. I was choking. I fainted.

When I regained consciousness, probably just a few minutes later, I found myself sitting on the pavement, leaning against a building. I saw Lala's alarmed face and maybe a dozen astonished-looking children around her, chattering excitedly in German. My suitcase was lying in the middle of the street. In the distance I saw two German military policemen, who must have been guarding the neighborhood, approaching rapidly, almost running in our direction. Instantly I recalled what had taken place and, mustering all my strength, got up with Lala's help, forcing a smile to my face. The police asked Lala what had happened and she explained that I had stumbled and fallen. They looked suspiciously at my suitcase and asked me to open it. Fortunately, my Communion picture was on top, and this put them at ease. They searched briefly and let us go on our way to the interview.

Although Lala had described my future employer, I was still somewhat shocked when I met Dr. Brabetz. I didn't know she was part of the military. She must have been in her late thirties, very tall, and overweight. She was wearing the uniform of a lieutenant in the German armed forces.

Her face looked coarse and severe. She wore no makeup. Her long blond hair was arranged in braids, which were rolled to form a tight chignon at the nape of her neck and fastened with heavy bobby pins. When I mustered the courage to look into her eyes, I noticed to my surprise that they were kind and friendly, inconsistent with her general appearance and the image of a Valkyrie she was evidently trying for.

When we entered she made a gesture with her right hand as if to raise it and say Heil Hitler. Remembering this kind of greeting was reserved for Germans, she gave me a warm handshake instead.

Dr. Brabetz was unmarried and shared her practice and her apartment with her sister Anita, who was also a dentist. I was to assist both of them in their lab work, keep the offices clean, and perform general messenger duties. My pay was minimal, but I would get a room in the large apartment they had converted into a laboratory and the special food-ration coupons given to the Poles employed by Germans. Because of the language barrier, the interview did not last very long. To my surprise, I understood almost everything she said. I must have learned something, after all, from reading those obituaries in the German newspapers!

I was aware that this job would mean a whole new set of adjustments for me. At thirteen I would have to live by myself in a large five-room apartment. I would also have to work six days a week on a job that would probably keep me on the streets a great deal of the time, continuously exposed. Despite having lived in Warsaw for several months, I didn't know my way around. Gibalski Street, where Mrs. Krawczyk lived, was in a workers' neighborhood on the periphery of the city, while my new job and living quarters were in the fashionable downtown area. There was, however, a bright spot in the new situation: my mother worked just one block away from Dr. Brabetz's office, and I could see her daily.

When the interview was over, Lala kissed me on the forehead with tears in her eyes, then left. I stayed with my boss for the rest of the afternoon, watching her work on patients. Dr. Brabetz was to show me my living quarters after she finished work. Her lab was in the same building she lived in. It was an elegant apartment house near her office, now occupied by German families, the only other Pole being the concierge. I was given a large room in the converted apartment. Two other rooms and the kitchen were used for dental work. Dr. Brabetz showed me around for a few minutes and left. I was alone.

I adjusted to my job easily. In the morning I had to clean up and report to Dr. Brabetz. Her assistant, Christine, would then send me on errands or ask me to help out in the office.

The high point of my day was my meeting with my mother. Since her boss didn't know of my existence in Warsaw (he too had been told that I lived in Krakow), I could not visit her. We would meet in the hallway of an apartment house and talk for a few minutes. She would bring me my lunch and dinner packed neatly in three glass containers, and I would return the empty ones from the day before. Mother's job was a real success; she was again as effective and competent as I remembered her having been in the period after my father was taken from us.

Herr Rockschmidt, her boss, was a tall, suave, and handsome bon vivant, a playboy. He worked very little, the office being managed by his Polish uncle. My mother was in charge of housekeeping and was given a nearly unlimited amount of money to cater the parties that were given almost daily. She shopped for food on the black market and prepared the most elaborate meals, which included caviar and champagne. Rockschmidt was exempt from military service because of his position as owner and director of a trucking company that carried supplies for the German army. This was a rather unusual exemption for a man in his early thirties at a time when the Germans, having suffered devastating losses on the Russian front, were expanding the draft age into the late fifties. To maintain this position, he had to befriend all the important military and Gestapo men in Warsaw. My mother's cooking, and her ability to obtain exquisite delicacies and drink in those days of shortages and widespread hunger, made Rockschmidt dependent on her. Stasia, as she was known (the diminutive of her assumed Christian name, Stanislawa), became the central figure of his Warsaw operation: a confidante sworn to secrecy, pledged not to say a word to his wife on her rare visits from their estate near Berlin.

Once more, I was witnessing an absurd situation created by the war.

My mother, the modest, sensitive, ladylike Jew, was almost playing the role of a madam, catering, meeting important Nazi officials, bossing her employer around. Strange as it may sound, mutual admiration was developing between her and Rockschmidt. He would introduce her to his Nazi friends as "my jewel," and he was the only one allowed to call her by her first name (the others had to address her as "Frau Stasia"). Mother, for her part, was impressed by his impeccable manners, his forty-odd hand-tailored suits and close to one hundred shirts. He also admitted to her privately that he was not a member of the Nazi party. My mother was maintaining the same kind of elegant household we had had before the war in Lwów. It was hard for me to reconcile all this with our real situation.

Rockschmidt's uncle – everyone called him "Wuja" which means "uncle" in Polish – vicariously enjoyed his nephew's carrying on.

Wuja was a very unusual, very special man. In his early sixties, with his gray hair in a crew cut, gentle blue eyes, and friendly smile, he dressed as his nephew. They had the same tailor, a Jew whom the Gestapo kept in their headquarters in Warsaw to make uniforms for the top echelons and suits for their friends. As a Pole, Wuja felt guilty working for his German relative, but he could not resist the temptations of the luxurious life in Warsaw. He had left his wife in a little town where he had been a minor railroad official and now was trying to assume the identity of a country squire displaced to the capital. He sought to act the wise and experienced gentleman, equally at ease in either place. Wuja didn't lack humor or insight. Frequently, after having made a major faux pas, he would complain to my mother, "How come at home they think I behave like a city gentleman, and here they call me a peasant?" Wuja had eighteen children.

He admired my mother and told her that he sensed she had not been a domestic before. He suspected that she was a Polish aristocrat in hiding for political reasons. He knew the former Polish military attaché in Berlin, Colonel Glowacki, and the fact that my mother's assumed maiden name was Glowacki, made him suspect her of being the colonel's daughter. My mother neither denied nor confirmed his suspicions. Wuja's speculations as to her provenance were positive additions to the image she was cultivating. They explained the disparity between my mother's looks and behavior and her job as a domestic.

Zosia wrote on several occasions that she felt lonely and insecure in Mogila, and was wondering if it would be possible for her and Marysia to come to Warsaw. Since Ludwig's death, we considered it our duty to assist Zosia. Because of Lala's exceptional knack for survival methods, we felt more capable of mastering difficult situations and thus be available to help others, especially Zosia.

Just as Ludwig had, Lala now became the central figure in our lives. It must have been the combination of their age (late teens, early twenties), intelligence, zest for life, flexibility, and the strength that allowed Ludwig and, later on, Lala to continually mastermind escape strategies that would have made Houdini jealous.

We discussed Zosia's letter on a Sunday in my mother's room. By then we had figured out a way for me to visit Mother on Sundays. (Lala was there officially as her niece.) I would sneak into my mother's tiny maid's room through the service entrance when Wuja was in church, spend the day there, sitting in the closet in case someone came in unexpectedly, and leave when Wuja was taking his afternoon nap. We relished those precious two hours on Sunday. It was the first time since the beginning of the war that we had been able to be together and feel completely safe. I would sit on a pillow in the closet with the door open, feasting on some exquisite pastry my mother had bought for me with her boss's money, while she and Lala lounged on the bed.

We had plenty to talk about: our jobs, our bosses, and the good news from the BBC. Lala had discovered the Jews working in disguise in Schmoll's lab, and became friendly with them. Together we poked fun at the stupid Nazi. Through our various contacts and chance encounters we had by then a small group of Jewish friends in Warsaw. Our occasional contacts with them were very important for our morale. Also, from a practical point of view, these Jewish friends were able to give us important ideas and assistance that might help us survive.

We decided to look for jobs as domestics for Zosia and Marysia. In what must have been one of her weaker moments, Lala suggested that I sell Dr. Brabetz on the idea that she needed a housekeeper and then propose Marysia for the job. I was ambivalent about the plan, remembering well Marysia's disastrous performance on her last job. But the idea of seeing her daily, maybe even sharing my room with her, was appealing. Selfishly, I accepted Lala's plan without expressing my doubts. To my surprise, Dr. Brabetz was amenable to my suggestion, and it didn't take much to convince her that Marysia would be an asset. Dr. Brabetz was already enjoying my services as a messenger boy; the thought of having another servant for so little money must have appealed to her. Zosia got a job through Wuja, working for five German civilians who shared an apartment.

To my surprise, I was enjoying my job very much. Both in the office and in the lab, I was learning new skills. In a short while Dr. Brabetz started to teach me how to model teeth for prostheses, which I found both interesting and satisfying. It was the first time in more than two years that I was being taught something, and I couldn't get enough of it.

I became friendly with Dr. Brabetz's assistant, Christine, who was nineteen and Volksdeutsche, a Pole of ethnic German origin. Her German was no better than mine. In fact I would occasionally help her out with German words when she couldn't explain something to one of our patients. She had a boyfriend in the German Army on the Russian front, and she never stopped quoting to me from his letters. I in turn, had to fabricate stories about my family in order to satisfy her seemingly limitless curiosity. It wasn't difficult, as my imagination was at its zenith, stimulated by age and by the experiences of the past two years. What did become a problem was remembering all that phantasmagoria, especially vis-a-vis Christine who, despite her limited intelligence and the inappropriateness of having a thirteen-year-old as a confidant, remembered every detail of what I had told her and was liable to ask for additional information weeks later.

Warsaw was a peculiar place to be in 1943. Four years of German occupation had forced its people to develop a style of living that seemed to have no historical precedent. A very small group cooperated openly with the Germans. These were the Polish policemen, the navy-blue police as they were called, in distinction to the green-uniformed German police. They were feared and despised by everyone, including, I think, the Germans. Being the Polish quislings, these traitors had placed themselves totally outside of Polish society, since all other Poles had always been virulently anti-German and were now anti-Nazi. Most of Warsaw's inhabitants were poor, struggling to make ends meet through black-market machinations and smuggling food into the city. There was, however, a small well-to-do elite drawing on savings from before the war and selling precious jewelry and works of art to the Germans. They lived in luxury and frequented fine restaurants and nightclubs – ironically, open only until 8:00 p.m. I was very surprised to see those places on my daily errands. I was particularly happy to find that there were also several theaters and movie houses open daily and offering relatively good fare.

As I had anticipated, Marysia's sojourn at Dr. Brabetz's was short. On the third day, she started a major fire while lighting the gas stove; she had – accidentally, I hope – lit the oil in the frying pan. We received a phone call from the concierge that the apartment was on fire and we arrived on the scene in a taxi, soon afterward. I was afraid that the dentist would blame me for Marysia – I was, after all the matchmaker – but she did not. Marysia was immediately fired. I told her to go to my mother, and she left without delay, looking unperturbed. She must have been relieved that the job was over. That night I felt more lonely than ever.

After the Marysia incident, my life remained uneventful for a while. Praying silently for things to remain as they were until the end of the war, I developed a routine. Morning errands for Dr. Brabetz were followed by lunch meetings with Mother, always at the same time, always in the same hallway. We exchanged a few words. I returned the empty jars and accepted the full ones and was on my way home. Afternoons meant a few more hours of work, then either home or a visit to Zosia until the eight o'clock curfew.

Then, suddenly, in November I nearly caused a disaster. It was Christine, Dr. Brabetz's dumb assistant, who almost did me in. We had continued the peculiar relationship in which I was her confidant. As in the past, I had to read every one of her boyfriend's letters and give my opinion as to whether he loved her and was still faithful to her. Wolfgang was now stationed in a small Russian town near the front lines, after having been slightly wounded. Christine was distressed by his mention, in several letters, of a nurse who took care of him in the hospital. It seemed to me, though, that her concern with fidelity was one-sided. I had observed, on several occasions, that she arrived at work in a Mercedes limousine driven by an elderly German officer. When I inquired about him, she blushed, was first at a loss for words, and then said that the man was her father's schoolmate who was now stationed in Warsaw. I did not comment, but she must have sensed that I didn't believe her. Having discovered her secret I now felt superior to her, despite the fact that she was nineteen and I was thirteen. I guess she was waiting to get back at me and jumped at the first opportunity. We were discussing the forthcoming Christmas holiday. I, in my ignorance of Christian holidays, remembering that Easter came late in 1943, asked "on what date does Christmas fall this year?"

She looked at me in complete disbelief. I sensed immediately that I had asked the wrong question. It was too late, however. She hesitated for a second and then said suspiciously, "So you don't know when Christmas is? You must then be a Jew! That makes sense... Now I know why you knew more German than I did: All Jews are international cosmopolitans. You run the Kremlin and Wall Street."

I was alarmed; her voice was vitriolic. Who would have thought that this dumb girl would be so fast to figure it all out? She even quoted from Der Stürmer, the German newspaper devoted entirely to anti-Semitism.

Denying the truth would be to no avail: I was at her mercy. After regaining my composure, my voice still trembling, I tried to appease her. It was lunchtime, and we were alone in the dentist's office. She did not respond to my pleading. She must have been very upset about having confided all the intimacies of her life to me. She wasn't talking to me anymore.

When Dr. Brabetz entered, she must have been surprised to see our faces flushed and our bodies rigid in our effort to contain our emotions. Typically, she made no comment. As in the incident with the fire caused by Marysia, she acted above it all: she must have taken her role as representative of the master race very seriously.

5

My Hitler Youth Uniform

The incident with Christine left me deeply shaken. I decided not to tell Mother and Lala about what had happened so as not to alarm them. I was pretty sure that Christine would keep her promise. I also knew that I had to stay at Dr. Brabetz's; there was nowhere else to go. In any case my boss was friendly with Dr. Schmoll, Lala's employer, who, in turn, knew Rockschmidt. Our fates were interlocked, and I had to maintain the status quo.

Christine quit rather unexpectedly, a week before Christmas. She volunteered as a nurse for the German army, hoping to be reunited with her Wolfgang. I thought she could not tolerate the tension that resulted from our encounter at the office. I was amused at the idea that I had inadvertently contributed to the German war effort.

Dr. Brabetz invited me to my first traditional Christmas dinner. She gave me a present that was to help me survive that winter in Warsaw and at one point save my life: a black skiing outfit, pants and jacket. When I tried it on it occurred to me that I looked as if I were wearing a Hitler Youth uniform. Almost all Germans my age belonged to the Hitler Jugend and wore black outfits not unlike the one I received from my boss. The only items I lacked were a few emblems and a swastika on my hat. I wore this suit to Dr. Brabetz's party, and to my delight, most of the guests assumed that I was her relative. For the first time in a long while I felt safe.

It was amazing how this unexpected gift changed the course of my life in Warsaw. I began riding in the section of the tram reserved exclusively for Germans and no one questioned me. This reinforced my feeling that I looked authentic. If they asked me for my Hitler Youth membership card, I planned to say I had left it at home. Not wearing the official emblems, I wasn't really pretending to be a member of the organization; I was simply capitalizing on the illusion created by the black outfit and the fact that most people usually pay no attention to details.

While I rode in the almost empty compartment, the Poles were squeezed like sardines in the rest of the tram. They stared at me with hatred, and I could barely contain my desire to laugh in their faces. I was contemplating the newest absurdity of my situation – being hated by the Poles not for being a Jew but for being a German. This new twist of fate gave me a great deal of satisfaction. I was fooling the whole world, Poles and Germans alike. I thought that if I survived the war I should become a spy; or maybe a diplomat.

Feeling secure on the streets, I started to explore Warsaw on my own. The city was fascinating, torn by contradictions. Germans and Poles: oppressors and victims. There were stores full of merchandise at prices that only a few could afford, while the majority starved; executions on street corners, while theaters and movie houses played to capacity audiences; elegant black Mercedeses side by side with horse-drawn droshkies and bicycle rickshaws; newsstands full of German papers which no one could read, while sought after information was hunted eagerly in the daily underground newsletter printed and distributed by the Armia Krajowa under the threat of execution. (Mietek, Mrs. Krawczyk's nephew, had supplied us daily with this.) I observed it all with a mixture of excitement and bewilderment, trying to sort out these impressions as they confronted me daily. Tantalized by all that was happening, I started to go to the movies and the theater on my own, at least once or twice a week. Mother and Lala thought I was out of my mind; they couldn't see how I had the curiosity and the peace of mind necessary to pursue these interests. Looking back, I really don't know what it was that allowed me so much control over my feelings while faced with daily threats to my life. Perhaps it was the experience of mastery over an unbelievably dangerous situation. I must have unconsciously enjoyed the fact that a nation of eighty million was trying to murder an innocent thirteen-year-old boy, and was unsuccessful. How could I help but feel omnipotent? Luckily, this sense of superiority didn't get out of hand. I maintained my good judgment and my ability to quickly assess imminent or potential danger.

Ironically, as the Russians were marching west against dwindling German opposition and the allies were winning in Italy, it was becoming almost as dangerous to be a Pole – especially a male Pole – in Warsaw as it was to be a Jew.

The Polish resistance was extremely active in the winter of 1944, and retaliatory street executions of Polish hostages by Germans occurred almost daily. In February, Mietek was executed on Marszalkowska, Warsaw's main street. We were very sad. Lala, who still lived on Gibalski Street, told us how Mietek, although very active in the underground, had been apprehended in a routine arrest of innocent passersby while walking to work one day. He was publicly executed the following day, together with nine other Poles. These executions became monuments for the resistance heroes. On the following day I went to place flowers in front of the bullet-riddled wall where Mietek had been gunned down. The pavement was still red with his blood. Someone had already affixed small plates with the names of the victims, each plate in the place where they stood facing the German firing squad. The square was filled with women and children, all sobbing uncontrollably. I couldn't keep from crying. As if before my eyes, I saw my father, his head pierced by a bullet, blood dripping down his cheeks like tears.

I stood there a long while. I was one of the mourners; I belonged there. It was the first time I had been able to cry for my father openly. But I felt very sad about Mietek as well. For me, he had symbolized the good in the Polish people. Surrounded by this sea of hostility and naked aggression, I could ill afford to lose one of the few decent Poles that I had encountered during the war. I would have stood there longer had I not suddenly spotted Mrs. Krawczyk and Edek in the crowd. She was all in black, her face half-covered with a black veil. Edek, looking very sad, with eyes swollen from crying, wore a black armband. Since Lala had told them I had gone back to Krakow, it wouldn't have been good for them to see me there. I turned and walked away, wishing I could talk to someone about what I had just experienced, but aware that I had to wait until the next day when I would see my mother. I didn't want to burden Zosia with my problems, knowing full well they would bring back painful memories of Ludwig. Despite the bitter cold of a February afternoon, I decided to walk home, hoping that the long walk would help me cope with my grief. I wished I could wear a black armband like Edek's to let the world know how hurt I was, but I knew that it would look incongruous on my Hitler Youth-like uniform. Survival comes first.

After Mietek's death, the winter was generally uneventful. Mother continued to work for Rockschmidt, her importance there growing every day. She had almost unlimited spending money, made all the decisions that pertained to housekeeping, and reached a point where she was rationing vodka for Rockschmidt's Uncle Wuja, who was becoming increasingly intimidated by Mother's decisiveness and self-assurance. It was somewhat the reverse of our home situation in Lwów: now she was the boss. Lala's position at Dr. Schmoll's was also solid. The German military misfortunes on all fronts alarmed the dentist, and he started to wear a white coat on top of his SS uniform. To Lala's amazement, he mentioned for the first time that he had worked before the war for a Jewish dentist in Hamburg. The dentist had immigrated to Palestine, and he wondered aloud whether his former boss was still alive. The shrewd fox was preparing an alibi for himself in anticipation of Hitler's demise. Mother and I were very excited when Lala told us about it. To us it meant that even the Nazi elite, to which Dr. Schmoll belonged, no longer believed in victory. Lala wrote down the name of the dentist in Palestine – planning, as she told us, to tell him after the war was over how Dr. Schmoll had behaved during the Nazi occupation.

We were sure now that we were going to survive. (Little did we know how much more we would have to endure.) We thought a great deal about our future after the war. Once we found Father, we planned to immigrate to Palestine where my grandparents and my father's brother and three sisters lived. From the beginning of the German occupation, Mother made us memorize my Aunt Pola's address in Tel Aviv: 5 Jabotinski Street. This was the place we were to meet after the war, if we were separated by unforeseen circumstances. The address had an air of magic for me. It was a talisman, important to hold on to; it symbolized a happier future, and, we hoped, reunion with Father. When things were very bad and danger imminent, I would suddenly become afraid that I might forget this address and never see anyone in my family again. As frightening as the thought may have been, it was, I guess, better than the more likely alternative: that they would never see me again, if the Germans killed me.

I often spent the long winter evenings alone in my room, daydreaming about the time when I would sit in my grandfather's living room in Tel Aviv telling all my aunts, uncles, and cousins about my war experiences. I knew each of them well: they had all immigrated to Palestine from Poland only a few years before the war.

In March, we celebrated my birthday for the first time since 1939. It was probably the most absurd event of the whole war. Wuja had gone away to spend the Easter holiday with his family, and Rockschmidt was in Germany. Mother decided to throw a big dinner party for all our Jewish friends and acquaintances hiding in Warsaw. I still find it hard to believe that it really happened. The audacity of the idea! A birthday party for a fourteen-year-old Jewish boy in the elegant and exclusive

German section of the city, in the apartment of a German businessman and financed with his money – all this in Warsaw in 1944! Our guest list included eleven people, and adding the three of us, Mother planned a dinner for fourteen. Because only Germans had access to telephones, Lala invited everyone personally. So as not to arouse the suspicion of the concierge in Rockschmidt's building, we gave everyone an exact arrival time that staggered their coming over a two-hour period. The night before the party I slept in Rockschmidt's apartment in his luxurious bed, satin sheets and all. We were very excited about our extravagant plan and schemed until late that night. Mother's dinner menu underscored the meaning and uniqueness of the event. Only Jewish ethnic foods were to be served. Gefilte fish would be followed by chopped liver, chicken soup and so on through the kichel for dessert – all financed by Herr Heinrich Rockschmidt.

The first one to arrive was Professor Zwilling, a well-known gynecologist from Lwów, my mother's doctor whom she had met by chance on the street in Warsaw. Professor Zwilling was now living in a rented room he rarely left. He pretended, for the sake of the gentile landlady, who didn't know that he was Jewish, that he was writing a medical textbook and didn't have time to go out. Before he left Lwów, the professor had had plastic surgery on his nose.

Professor Zwilling was suave and eloquent. He reminded me of Dr. Landau, my father's friend and member of his "war cabinet." Like Dr. Landau, he quoted Latin freely, from Ovid to Tacitus, and he interspersed his comments with anecdotes from the time he had been a physician at the court of Emperor Franz Joseph of Austro-Hungary during World War I. This was only the third time I had seen him, and I had been eagerly looking forward to his arrival. His presence brought back precious memories of the time when my father was still with us.

Mrs. Schotzler came next, with her old mother. She was the widow of a very prominent and wealthy banker from Lwów; under normal circumstances, she would not have socialized with my mother since we were not nearly wealthy enough for her. They knew each other from the PTA of my school, and had met accidentally in my mother's neighborhood in Warsaw. Mrs. Schotzler was also working as a domestic. I surmised from the way she and her mother were dressed when they arrived at our party that she must have escaped from Lwów with a lot of money. I looked in disbelief at her opulent black karakul fur adorned with a silver fox collar. Both women wore diamond necklaces of exceptional size and beauty. Wasn't she concerned about being seen by her employer? Mrs. Schotzler had escaped the Janowski Detention camp in Lwów after having bribed a German guard with several large diamond bracelets which (she claimed) were worth close to half a million dollars. Her husband and her son had been released along with her, but the guard had shot them all in the back after letting them leave the camp. Mrs. Schotzler had managed to survive by falling to the ground after being shot at and pretending to be dead until nightfall. Now she lived with her mother in a rented room. Her mother, who didn't know Polish very well and spoke mainly Yiddish, pretended to be deaf and dumb. She hadn't talked to anyone, not even to her daughter for the past two years.

Zosia and Marysia were next. After a fifteen-minute interval they were followed by the Kramers, now the Zapolskis, the only intact family we knew in Warsaw. They came with their six-year-old-son Jurek, now called Maria, he was pretending to be a girl. We were all amazed how, at six, he was capable of acting and behaving like a girl. In comparison to his achievements at six, mine at thirteen seemed almost trivial. I hadn't seen him before. I had only heard about him from Lala. His father was a dental technician in Dr. Schmoll's office. I looked in disbelief at the pixieish little girl with braided blond hair and lively cheerful eyes. He was wearing a frilly white dress and red leotards. I didn't know how to behave, how to address him, Jurek? Maria? I chose to avoid him altogether. It was too much for me to cope with. What a birthday party!

There were two more people to complete the list: Kazik, Tadzio's friend, and his wife Irka. Kazik was different from us all. As though it weren't enough that he was a Jew in hiding, he was also a member of the resistance.

Despite their all-out war with the Germans, the National Resistance Army – the Armia Krajowa – accepted Jews into its ranks only with great reluctance. (Most of the Poles weren't fighting Nazism, I think; they were fighting Germany, their ancient foe, and therefore remained comfortably anti-Semitic while shedding their own blood in the resistance war.)

The Jews in the underground, therefore, belonged to a splinter resistance group, the People's Army – the Armia Ludowa – which represented the leftist and communist Poles and eagerly welcomed Jews into their midst. Many of the Polish guerrilla forces – the so-called partisans that were using the vast Polish forests as their headquarters and fighting grounds – belonged to the people's Army. While the Armia Krajowa was basically a part-time outfit – its members lived at home –

the People's Army was a full-time resistance force that, in addition to fighting, offered a hiding place, a shelter to the Jews.

To many Poles, however, the Armia Krajowa's neutral attitude toward Jews was unsatisfactory. They felt that hating the Germans should not prevent them from hating the Jews. They formed a third, rightist resistance group that was simultaneously fighting the Germans and the Jews, mostly those in the woods. (Resistance, Polish style: help the enemy you fight.)

A unit of Armia Ludowa in the Polish forest.

Of course, Kazik belonged to the People's Army. He had a fascinating but dangerous assignment: he was an engineer for the underground radio station that maintained contact between the army's headquarters and Moscow. The Germans had somehow managed to track down the source of the radio waves and had captured several of Kazik's predecessors together with precious equipment that was almost impossible to replace during the war. Kazik had developed an ingenious mobile radio transmitter that was embedded in the bottom of a pushcart. This permitted daily changes of locale, and for almost a year now the operation had been successful; the Germans had failed to detect the source of the transmissions that were hurting their war effort.

Kazik's assigned arrival time was 2:45 p.m., but by 3:15 there was no sign of him or his wife Irka. Professor Zwilling tried to entertain us but to no avail – no one was paying attention. The tension was unbearable. Mother and Lala were at the windows, looking out for Kazik and his wife or some unusual occurrence on the street. Tadzio recalled that on Sunday mornings Kazik's station transmitted to Moscow: Maybe he had been caught this time. Typically, Marysia expressed what was on all our minds. Maybe the concierge, noticing the unusual number of people arriving in Rockschmidt's absence, had reported this to the police, and Kazik had been the first one apprehended. We would now be arrested any minute. Hearing this, the Zapolskis got up and said that they wanted to leave immediately. Mrs. Schotzler's mother started to sob uncontrollably, clinging to her daughter like a little baby.

Everyone was shouting at the top of their lungs. I looked at my mother, who was pale and shaken. I knew she was blaming herself for having imperiled the lives of all those people. I saw her go over to Professor Zwilling and talk to him in an agitated voice. In the pandemonium around me I couldn't understand what she was saying. The professor was disagreeing with her, shaking his head vigorously. Mother was no longer paying attention to him. She went to the hallway and started to put on her coat. This silenced everyone. With her voice trembling and tears rolling down her cheeks, she announced that as all this was her fault, she would have to bear the consequences. She would go down to the concierge, and if the police were there she would try to hold them off long enough for us to get out through the service entrance and the fire escape staircase. "Don't try to stop me," she continued, now calm and determined. "I have to go."

As she headed toward the door, the doorbell rang. We froze. There was no choice now but to open the door. It was too late. We had missed our chance. Mother looked at us; hesitated for a second; and then, gathering all her courage, opened the door. It was Kazik. He was surprised to see us all standing in a frozen position facing the door, our eyes filled with fear. After we all calmed down, Lala explained to him what had happened. Kazik, in turn, gave us his reasons for being so late.

After the morning broadcast, he had gone to fetch Irka from the church. Irka, who looked very Jewish, had spent the last year and a half hiding in a church. She would arrive early in the morning for the morning mass and stay there until it was dark, pretending to pray. We wondered whether she was still merely pretending after such a long time. From what she said, we deduced that she was starting to see herself as a Catholic. She had even said openly once that she had to thank Mary for saving her life. It was an ambiguous statement. We weren't sure whether she meant that by hiding in a church she'd been saved, or that she'd been saved by a miracle. No one dared ask for clarification.

Kazik reported that Irka had refused to come to our party. He had spent the intervening time trying to convince her to come, but to no avail. Once more it wasn't clear whether she was afraid to lose her cover, or if she felt that she had to be in church because this was Palm Sunday.

Our mood changed dramatically within seconds. Professor Zwilling proposed a toast and, forgoing his Latin, said in Hebrew, "Leshana habah b'Yerushalaim – Next year in Jerusalem." He commented that this was the time of year of Passover; as the Jews in ancient Egypt were freed from their slavery, so would we survive Hitler and live to enjoy freedom and peace. Now everyone was crying, gulping the vodka my mother was pouring into large glasses. Despite the ominous beginning, the party turned out to be an amazing success, everyone truly having a great time. I think it was partly due to our ability to recover rapidly – within minutes – from the most painful and traumatic experience, and partly due to the fact that all the men were drunk. The highlight of the day was the news in Polish, from the BBC in London, which we all listened to on Rockschmidt's radio. It was very good. The Allies were preparing an invasion of Europe: the war couldn't last much longer.

I sighed with relief when Mother closed the door after the last guest had left. This was not the time to have a birthday party.

The spring of 1944 started uneventfully for all of us. It was obvious by then that the Germans had lost the war. It was only a question of time – months or maybe only weeks – until the Russians took Warsaw. There were rumors that the Allies were planning an invasion of France around the end of April, when the weather got a little warmer. We had a great deal of contact with the Germans: Lala with Dr. Schmoll, Mother with Rockschmidt, Zosia with her employer, and I with Dr. Brabetz. This kept us in touch with the latest developments and we were able to check the attitude among the Nazis before formal announcements were made on the radio. To the end, the official communiqués from the headquarters of the German army were masterpieces of propaganda. Ambiguous statements, replete with euphemisms: a defeat on the battlefields was described as a "strategic retreat"; a retreat was a "consolidation of the front line." Had it not been for the BBC and daily encounters with our employers, it would have been impossible to assess what was really going on.

Zosia's bosses were the first to leave Warsaw. She was the housekeeper for five German executives who were in charge of the civilian administration of Warsaw. Their departure was significant to us; it hinted that the Nazis were quitting. Having failed on the front, the Germans were now retaliating viciously against the Polish civilian population. It was becoming dangerous for a Polish male to walk the streets; daily raids were followed by mass street executions like the one in which Mietek had perished. Being preoccupied with my Jewishness, I had never placed myself in the category of a vulnerable Polish male, and had been traveling daily all over the city, relieved that the pressure was off the Jews. This was obviously a mistake, a narrow point of view which nearly had disastrous consequences.

It was late in April. I was on one of my errands for Dr. Brabetz, walking on Warsaw's main street, the Marszlkowska. Suddenly, without any warning, people on the sidewalk – mostly men – started running in all directions, trying to get into buildings along the streets. A few seconds later, I saw German military police jumping off trucks in pursuit of escaping pedestrians. I looked around, very frightened, and realized that the street was blocked off by German army trucks. Each building's entrance was guarded by a Gestapo man, his sub-machine gun aimed at the panic-stricken pedestrians.

I knew I was trapped. They were taking men for tomorrow's public execution. I was somewhere in the middle, about a block away from either barricaded exit of the surrounded street, and I had to move. Where to? I stalled for time. The first men were already being loaded onto death trucks, their hands above their heads. The Germans were hitting brutally with their rifle butts. I heard shots very close to me. I ran a few steps and pressed as close as I could against the wall of a building, trying to melt into it. A man fell to the ground, face down, some ten feet away from me, blood gushing from his neck. He had tried to escape and had been shot, point-blank. I continued walking, not wanting to attract attention to myself. I hesitated for an instant when I had to step into a puddle of blood now surrounding the fallen man but then proceeded, my heart pounding, as if nothing had happened. My shoes were splattered with blood. A moment later I spotted two German army women walking briskly toward the barricade, probably to get out of the now-dangerous area in which they had been accidentally trapped.

Seeing the two uniformed women suddenly reminded me that I was still wearing my pseudo-Hitler Youth uniform, the snowsuit I had gotten from Dr. Brabetz for Christmas. It was a cold April, and I had tried to stretch the protective value of this outfit as long as possible. In the panic of the events of the past few minutes, I hadn't considered the uniform. I had associated this garb with covering up my Jewishness and hadn't psychologically prepared to be endangered as a Pole! Ironically, in the four years of war, this was the closest I had come to being apprehended and killed.

Another instant and I had a rescue plan. I joined the fast-walking women and, without stopping them, asked in German for directions to the German YMCA. The three of us were now walking briskly, engaged in a conversation, both women trying to explain to me how to get there. A minute later we walked by the barricade, with the Gestapo police saluting us with a forced grin, assuming that we were three Germans walking together. I glanced out of the corner of my eye at the almost full truckload of bleeding, doomed men. They had the same horror-stricken eyes that haunted me since I saw the train of Jews being carried to death in Auschwitz two years earlier. The two German women looked stunned when I left them abruptly in the middle of a sentence once we crossed the barricade. I didn't care. I had to get away from it all, fast. It was more than I could take.

I thought that I had become tougher, more immune to danger in those years of underground existence, but I realized suddenly that nothing can really prepare one for death. Those few minutes were the most frightening I had ever experienced. Had it not been for my quick thinking I would have been shot to death like Mietek within the next twelve hours. The trucks were leaving now. They were filled with men, innocent passersby. There was silence on the street. People were crossing themselves, their eyes on the condemned men. I felt faint and nauseated. I decided not to go on with the errand for Dr. Brabetz but to go to Zosia, the one person I could visit during the day. Luckily I had a few zlotys on me, so I could take a bicycle rickshaw, the only means of private transportation in those days. The Polish rickshaw driver looked somewhat perplexed when I approached him. The picture of a pale, frightened, crying Hitler Youth member must have been a novelty for him, but once I showed him that I had the fare he drove me to my destination without asking questions.

Zosia was alarmed when she saw me. From the way I looked and the odd hour of my visit – it was noon and I had never visited her before four, when Dr. Brabetz closed the office – she sensed that something terrible must have happened. I didn't say a word, just went into the bathroom to vomit. I lay down on Zosia's bed in a tiny maid's room and stopped shivering only after she had covered me with two or three blankets. An hour later I tried to get up for my daily rendezvous with Mother, but I couldn't. I felt faint. Zosia went instead, and they both came back half an hour later. My mother was in shock: her face was pale, colorless. She had fainted when she saw Zosia instead of me arriving in the hallway where we always met. She had been sure that I was caught, and that Zosia had come to tell her.

I stayed at Zosia's that night, afraid to be alone. Although Dr. Brabetz's new maid, Kasia, was now living in my apartment, I hardly knew her and certainly could not share my experiences of the past day with her.

Not surprisingly, I couldn't fall asleep that night. All night long I saw the bleeding man and tried to imagine his face. Had I seen him before he was shot? When I finally fell asleep, I dreamed of my father. I was walking on the street – it looked like Lwów, but I wasn't sure – when suddenly I saw my father strolling in my direction. He was peculiarly dressed in pajamas, over which he wore his elegant blue winter coat with its fancy beaver collar. His head was shaved. He was half a block from me when I spotted him and started to run toward him. I must have been ten feet away when a shot rang out and I saw my father fall on his back, blood trickling from his forehead, his arms spread. I woke up and saw Zosia bending over my bed, looking helpless. She said that I had been shouting and crying in my sleep all night.

I slept late the following morning. When I got up I felt fine, ready to go back to work, embarrassed for having lost control the day before. I wondered whether the fact that I might have been caught because I was a "Pole" accounted for the intensity of my reaction. It was a new twist in my situation, an additional danger for which I was unprepared.

Fortunately, Dr. Brabetz's practice was dwindling rapidly and there were almost no errands to run. While the Germans were packing, the rest of us were rejoicing. Dr. Schmoll sent all his fancy dental equipment back to Hamburg. Ironically, he asked Lala a favor: to intercede for him with Rockschmidt so that he could get space on one of Rockschmidt's trucks. This was one favor that she did for him with pleasure, even enthusiastically. We were all ready to help them pack. We waited four very long years for this moment.

Dr. Brabetz and her sister stopped wearing their army uniforms. I was now invited for dinner with them almost every night. Kasia, their maid, was also asked to sit at the table. My boss's boyfriend was in Germany, where he was having a prostheses fitted for his amputated legs. For the first time since I had met them, the sisters mentioned that they were part Czech, having been born and raised in the part of Czechoslovakia called Sudeten Deutschland. Even their last name was Czech if you spelled it differently; Brabec. They also spoke the language; and because Slavic languages are similar, they understood Polish as well.

This really infuriated me. All those months when Christina and I had been trying to make ourselves understood in our marginal, broken German, those tight-lipped sisters had given us no inkling that they might understand Polish. Now, faced with defeat, frightened about their future they were suddenly becoming human, claiming to be like us. They couldn't fool me! Although they hadn't done me any personal wrong, I was determined that once the war was over all the Germans would be held responsible and pay for their compatriots' crimes – they were all collaborators. As Professor Zwilling had said once, "A good German deserves a good death, and a bad German a bad death."

After dinner, upstairs, we continued to poke fun at the two pathetic, frightened Nazi sisters. Kasia wasn't very interested in who was held accountable for the war. She was a rather simple country girl, seventeen or eighteen years old, but seeing my enthusiasm, she went along with my plans for revenge. Like Christine and Marysia in the past, she treated me as if I were older than fourteen, at least her age, if not more. After an initial period of mutual shyness, we were rapidly becoming very friendly.

6

The Warsaw Uprising

The summer of 1944 was the best in five years for me. Dr. Brabetz left in June, tears in her eyes. She gave me her address in Bratislava, and I had to promise to visit her after the war. She said she hoped I would grow up to be a dentist and use the experience I had gained in her laboratory to my advantage. Dr. Schmoll was the next to go. He left at night, without saying goodbye. He took everything with him except the portraits of Hitler that were left hanging in each of the many treatment rooms in his office.

Herr Rockschmidt played the role of a gentleman to the very end. His wife Berta arrived from their estate near Berlin to help pack, but an order by the German military forbade the use of trucks to transfer personal belongings back to Germany. The equipment was needed to move the military supplies of the retreating armies. Rockschmidt gave my mother all the furniture and household goods as a "present … in appreciation for your devotion." Mrs. Rockschmidt was the only German we had met who rejoiced at the fact that the Nazis were losing. It was for personal reasons, to be sure. She told Mother that now the war was coming to an end she would get her husband back. "Now it's the end to "der Grosse Herr" and back to little Hansi," she said with a vindictive twinkle in her eyes. "I always knew he would be back. It was only a question of time." Hitler's defeat was turning into a personal victory: the return of the prodigal son.

We shared Mrs. Rockschmidt's satisfaction, but for different reasons. It was hard to believe that the end of this terrible war would find us living better than when it had begun. Rockschmidt's apartment consisted of five large rooms lavishly furnished with modern and antique furniture of unknown, probably Jewish provenance. We doubted that he had bought this furniture. It had probably been "requisitioned" somewhere in occupied Europe by his Gestapo friends, the way Major Kedves had "borrowed" our belongings back in Lwów. It felt as if a circle was closing. Justice after all?

Mother suggested that I now move into the apartment. This immediately put me in a quandary; I didn't want to leave Kasia. Mother didn't know of Kasia's existence, and I had to lie in order to convince her that it wouldn't be a good idea to move now. I told her that it wasn't safe for us to live together as long as the Germans were still in Warsaw. I felt a little guilty lying to her, but I had changed in those five years of war. I had become very self-protective, even selfish. I thought I had suffered enough and should have a chance to have some fun for a change.

Although Mother accepted my story, the decision to stay with Kasia brought its own danger. A week later, the concierge of my apartment house asked me – politely, of course – why I hadn't left with my aunt, Dr. Brabetz. At first, I didn't understand, but then I saw what he meant. He must have assumed that I was a German-Volksdeutsche, an ethnic German, and taken my outfit for an authentic Hitler Youth uniform. He seemed to be convinced of this; it was an impression based on a year's observation, after all.

To reveal my true identity was out of the question, too dangerous even in these last days of German occupation. After a few seconds of hemming and hawing, I stuttered, "Dr. Brabetz left me here to watch her lab... She's coming back soon, in a couple of days, as a matter of fact; to take the equipment and me back to the Reich." I thanked him for his concern.

He seemed to be angry, almost belligerent, under his façade of civility. I had learned in those years never to underestimate a Pole's propensity for violence. He wanted all the Germans to leave – immediately. I could understand that! For me, it was another first. Again, I was suddenly in danger, this time on suspicion of being a German. It was a retroactive compliment on how successful my cover was, but that didn't matter now. After having almost been killed as a Pole just a few weeks before, I couldn't take another chance. I had to move.

We had a beautiful view of Warsaw from Mother's apartment. At night we could see lights from explosions of bombs and artillery shells on the front lines, now not more than thirty or forty kilometers away from the city. The Russians were using their new weapon, the Katusha, a thirty-round mortar, and we would often count the number of explosions to confirm the weapon's effectiveness. We remembered their inefficiency at the beginning of the war and hoped they had overcome it.

The BBC commentator described at length the joint impact of the allied invasion of Normandy and the new Soviet offensive. Germany's eastern and western fronts were crumbling, and it was estimated that Warsaw would fall sometime in early August. The Germans were building fortifications all over the city, and we were waiting each day for more news, which we knew this time would be good. The liberation of Lwów, my hometown, had already been announced several months earlier, and I envied the people who had stayed behind. They were already free.

In March the Russians had established a Polish communist government in Lublin, a city in western Poland they had liberated. This made the Poles in Warsaw very unhappy. They saw the Polish exile government in London, although more than a thousand miles away, as their only true representative, and the much nearer communist government in Lublin as an imposed one. Rumor had it that there would be an uprising against the Germans in Warsaw in order to prove to the Russians that the Poles were capable of liberating their capital without outside help. They would show the world that the people's loyalties were with their leaders in London. We didn't take these rumors seriously. It seemed ridiculous to endanger the lives of a million people to prove a political point. It was clear to us that after Yalta, the Soviet presence was an inescapable political reality in this part of the world. Once more, we had underestimated the Polish mentality.

August 1, 1944; it was a beautiful summer afternoon. I was visiting with Zosia and Marysia, talking as usual about our plans for after the war. Mother was at home and Lala was visiting Kazik and Irka in the Old City. Marysia went out on an errand, but returned a few minutes later, pale and agitated. She said that the streets were empty and one could hear machine-gun fire and explosions of mortar shells in the distance. I thought perhaps the Russians had made a surprise attack, possibly parachuted into Warsaw. But Marysia had a different story; she had been told by someone on the street that this was the beginning of the uprising. I was stunned. How foolish could they be? Why now, just days before the Russians were to come? Knowing Marysia's propensity for exaggeration, I thought (or hoped) for a short while that she had blown the story out of proportion.

She hadn't. Minutes later, the air-raid sirens were blasting. We all rushed from Zosia's second-floor apartment down to the cellar, our air-raid shelter. The place was humming with people; everyone was agitated, and there were rumors galore. One fact was certain: it was an uprising. It had begun an hour earlier, initiated by the Armia Krajowa. The commander-in-chief was General Bor-Komorowski (this was an underground pseudonym). The uprising had started simultaneously in all the boroughs of Warsaw; its success was resounding according to the first, occasionally ambiguous reports. The Germans were fleeing. Large quantities of arms and ammunition, and even several tanks, had been captured by the insurgents. Victory was at hand. In a day or two it would all be over.

Someone made a toast to the liberated and free Poland. We all got up in the cramped cellar and started singing the Polish national anthem, "Poland hasn't perished yet, as long as we live..." Tears were streaming down some people's cheeks. It was time to rejoice. I was sorry that Mother and Lala were not with me at this great moment, the moment we had eagerly awaited through the long years of captivity. I couldn't believe it had really happened. I wanted to jump, to shout, "we made it, we made it!" but somehow felt that this wasn't the place to do it. Distrust of the Poles, or for that matter, any strangers, had become second nature by then, and I realized that a personal celebration could wait. At this point it had to be secret, in my own heart, like so many events of this war.

I glanced at Zosia. She didn't look happy at all. She was staring into space. I knew that she was thinking of Ludwig, her son, who hadn't made it. I wanted to go over and tell her that she should be proud to be the mother of a true hero. But I knew that saying this would not console her. I went over to her side and squeezed her hand. From her look, I could tell that she knew I understood. I felt a sudden urge to be with my mother and decided to run over to her place as soon as the raid was called off.

The first bomb exploded before we had finished the anthem. The building shook vigorously but didn't collapse. It was not a direct hit; the bomb must have struck next door. Very close. Our heads were covered with white dust from the ceiling plaster that had been loosened by the force of the explosion. The jubilation in the air-raid shelter changed instantly to tension. There were several further explosions at a greater distance, and then silence.

We stayed in the cellar awhile longer, but as there was neither a siren to call off the raid nor any more explosions, we slowly filed out of the shelter into the street. The building to the left of us was almost demolished. The front half had been torn off by the explosion; one could see rooms with furniture, pots on stoves, wardrobes full of clothes, doors ajar, just as they had been minutes before when their inhabitants had left their apartments to hide in the shelter. It looked like a huge open doll house.

No one seemed to be hurt; all must have gotten out in time. A cat was hiding in a corner of a half-demolished room on the third floor. It looked very frightened, flush against the wall, fearing to leave the little space it had. Then I heard a woman shout, "A crib, a crib!" Everyone froze. She pointed to an apartment on the second floor in the front of the bombed structure. A child's room with blue walls was untouched except for the missing front wall. In the left-hand corner, snug against the wall, stood a small wicker cradle. It seemed from where we stood that it was rocking. Someone in the crowd said that he could hear a baby crying. The crib kept rocking, but it seemed to me that this was due to the wind now blowing into the open room. There was a hushed silence; everyone strained to hear. I couldn't hear anything, but Marysia claimed that the baby was crying. The crib was now definitely in motion. People were asking the whereabouts of the baby's mother, but she was nowhere around. Someone volunteered to climb up to rescue the baby. It was a dangerous mission; there was really no way to get there and it was impossible to predict which part of the building would cave in when pressure was put on it. A young Pole in overalls started to scale the wall. The crowd watched in silence, everyone holding his breath, oblivious to the machine-gun fire that could be heard now distinctly. The man had hardly made it to the mezzanine when the crib started to shake rather vigorously. To everyone's surprise a large gray cat climbed out of the crib, tilting it so that we could see it was empty! The crowd burst out laughing hysterically, applauding the brave young man, glad he didn't have to undertake this dangerous mission.

I went up to Zosia's apartment to call Mother and tell her to expect me in a few minutes. She lived only five blocks away. I hardly recognized Mother's voice on the phone. She sounded extremely alarmed. Just a few blocks away, she had a very different picture of our situation. She claimed that her street and the whole German section had been cut off from the rest of the downtown area. The German YMCA just around the corner from Rockschmidt's apartment had become a German stronghold, with machine guns in windows barricaded with sandbags and light mortars on the roof. The Germans had repelled all the Polish insurgents' attempts to conquer the building, and the street in front of the Y, in full view of Mother's window, was covered with dead or dying Polish Resistance fighters. No one dared to pick up the casualties, as the Nazi snipers on the adjoining rooftops shot anyone in view. Mother forbade me to leave Zosia's place.

Lala had called her just a few minutes earlier. She too was cut off, staying at Kazik's in the Old City, which was in Polish hands but surrounded by the German army and without any direct contact with the rest of Warsaw. Fortunately, the phones were still working. We could maintain contact with one another.

I hung up the phone with a heavy heart. What luck! Just when everything was so good and hopeful, the situation had to take such a turn for the worse. Mother's description of the YMCA sounded ominous. I knew it was not her style to exaggerate. This, on top of the news that she and Lala were completely surrounded and cut off from each other, made me think that we had underestimated German strength. The mortally wounded dragon still had clout; the war wasn't over yet.

We went to the shelter twice that night, awakened by the air-raid sirens. The Germans had total control of the skies, because the resistance forces had no antiaircraft artillery. The Stuka bombers of the Luftwaffe, their insignia clearly visible, were now systematically, every hour or so, bombing a series of houses, street after street, flying extremely low in order to aim well and not hit their own positions just blocks away from ours.

The next day the sirens were silent; they were of no use. The bombardment was continuous, day and night. We all moved to the cramped cellar, each family being assigned a small area, enough for a mattress or two. We stayed there most of the time, with only short interruptions to get food from the apartment above.

Mother did not have to move to the shelter. Her neighborhood was still under German control, and bombs were not falling there. We maintained our telephone contact for two days, after which the Germans cut the lines to prevent communication between the various sections of the city. I was cut off from Mother and Lala when I least expected it.

On the fourth day of the uprising, we got the first hints of what had really happened. The command of the Armia Krajowa, the national Resistance Army, had started the open uprising against the German forces in Warsaw on August 1, at 5:00 p.m. They had done so without consulting the Russian military command headed by General Rokossovski, although the Soviet army was only twenty-five miles or so from the Polish capital. They did, however have the approval of the Polish exile government in London, a thousand miles away. The Allied forces in Western Europe gave the uprising only tacit consent, questioning the wisdom and necessity of this move in view of the imminent Soviet entry into Warsaw.

I shuddered, hearing about the political connotation of this move: a fight against Germany to score an advantage against the Russians. I knew the Soviets. I had experienced them just three years earlier. They didn't like to be crossed in their plans; they were suspicious and couldn't be outwitted – certainly not by the Poles! I was worried. Very worried.

The military picture was less clear. The resistance forces had made many important gains. Some sections of the city were completely liberated. The Old City was totally cut off; although under Polish rule, it was surrounded by the German army commanded by General Stahel. Our area, the so-called inner city, was militarily mixed. There were pockets of German resistance in several places, the YMCA near my mother being among the most important. Several of the German strongholds had been conquered, at a very high price in human lives; others continued to ward off repeated attacks. German snipers were becoming a real menace. They hid in places difficult to detect, mostly on rooftops, which made walking the streets dangerous, if not impossible.

The main concern of the Polish resistance, of all of us, was the continuous air raids by a relatively small number of German planes, which were systematically demolishing house after house, street after street. We were completely unprotected, with no antiaircraft guns or planes. The enemy bombers roamed the skies with impunity. Although the Polish underground army had amassed weapons and ammunition during the German occupation, supplies were dwindling rapidly in the fierce and bloody fighting. The formerly underground newspapers now became official. We read the detailed reports of various battles raging around the city. Rumor had it that although the Poles had over fifty thousand underground soldiers, their arms were at a ridiculously low level; one thousand rifles, two thousand hand guns, sixty-seven machine guns. Thirty-five antitank mortars, and twenty-five thousand hand grenades. Ammunition was also in very short supply. Only one in twenty-five soldiers, it seemed, was armed. The German army in Warsaw, although smaller, was armed from head to toe. It was also supported by tanks, artillery, and the air force.

We were told that the Allies in the west had promised to parachute in arms in a day or two. One of our neighbors in the cellar questioned the feasibility of this move. We were so far from the western supply lines it seemed almost impossible that planes would be capable of flying such a distance with heavy loads and without refueling. We knew of the existence of the Flying Fortresses, but no details of their capabilities were available. For obvious reasons, the Soviets had not been contacted yet, and as expected, they were not volunteering help.

I have to admit that the first week of the uprising was exciting. Despite the dangerous bombings and shootings, the general mood was one of exhilaration. The newspapers were filled with accounts of heroic deeds. The bravery of the Polish soldiers had always been legendary. Now, after five years of occupation and oppression, it seemed to have reached its zenith. No mission was too dangerous: no odds impossible to overcome. Even the Germans were admitting to heavy losses in men and weapons. There was no doubt that the uprising was hurting their war effort.

Toward the end of the week, I saw the first German prisoners of war. They had been caught when the Poles conquered the heavily-guarded Central Post Office. I was told by a neighbor that there were fifty or sixty of them, and that they were being kept under guard in a nearby school. Without telling Zosia, I left the shelter during a short interval between the bombing and went to look at the Germans. I couldn't resist seeing them defeated and humiliated. When I arrived at the school I was told that they were nearby, digging defense ditches for the Polish resistance forces. I found them a short while later. The Germans looked worse than I had expected: maybe it was the dramatic change from the self-assured "Herrenrasse" to the look of a war prisoner that I was not prepared for. They were haggard, dirty, and unshaven, sweating profusely in the warm August sun. Dozens of Polish civilians were watching them work and making derogatory comments. The Germans seemed frightened by the hostile crowd and worked diligently, without interruption, digging a trench across the street. The faces of all the frightening Nazis I had encountered since 1941 flashed before my eyes: Major Kedves, the German officers on the train to Krakow, Dr. Schmoll. I was tempted to see whether any of them were down there in the ditch, but realizing the absurdity of the fantasy, I returned home; Zosia might be worried about my disappearance. Still, I was thrilled. It must have been one of my happiest experiences in the whole war. What a day! What a victory!

The situation remained more or less stable during the second week of the rebellion. The British air force sent several planes, which parachuted in some badly needed weapons and ammunition. This was encouraging. Although we had expected more help, we were pleased with whatever was available. The Russians continued to ignore the uprising, as if we didn't exist. Becoming aware of the political and anti-Soviet aspect of the fighting, they were obviously reluctant to help.

The isolated Old City was fighting fiercely for its survival. Casualties were heavy. Knowing Lala wouldn't sit still, I was worried that she might get hurt. I assumed that Mother was all right: I could observe her neighborhood from the top of our building. I would go up on the roof and lying flat on my stomach lest I be detected by a German sniper, could see the house where she lived, just a few short blocks away. It was intact, safely contained. The YMCA building in the immediate neighborhood looked like a fortress, with windows either shattered or totally barricaded by sandbags. There were so many shell holes all over the building's façade that I wondered what made it stand up.

The view from my lookout post was eerie as a De Chirico painting. Empty streets were covered with rubble and shattered glass. Many buildings were nearly demolished or burned out; others were untouched, miraculously preserved, with window boxes full of lush, sun-soaked, late-summer flowers. Trenches cut through the streets, and above the trenches were barricades of strange conglomerates of material: overturned trolley cars, burned-out armored vehicles, sandbags, cobblestones, furniture. An occasional person crossed rapidly in a bent down position, or bent down, sometimes crawled in the trenches from one side of the street to the other. Machine-gun fire came in paroxysmal outbursts from various directions, punctuated by short periods of ominous silence or explosions of hand grenades and mortars.

I could spend hours lying there alone on the tin roof, basking in the warm sun. It was such an unusual experience, this bird's-eye view of a raging holocaust, that despite all the terrible events I had been exposed to during the last five years, I was spellbound. As usual I was wondering whether I still had a chance to survive. Did being here mean I had reached a point of no return? Such thoughts were regularly interrupted, rather abruptly, by the appearance on the horizon of one or more German bombers. I would hardly make it to the cellar before the first bombs started exploding. By then it was like Russian roulette: when the bomb didn't hit our building, we would be safe for a couple of hours, until the next planes arrived.

I got my first news from Lala on the tenth day. She sent a letter to me by courier, a friend of hers who got through from the Old City by walking underground in the sewer system. Lala was jubilant. She was actively involved in the war effort. "Irka and I," she wrote, "are working as medics, day and night. The casualties are massive but our spirits are high: we are fighting for freedom. Our forces in the Old City have freed a group of Greek Jewish prisoners of war from the Pawiak jail, and whenever we have a free moment, Irka and I are collecting food and clothing for the prisoners, who are undernourished and have only striped jail uniforms to wear." According to the letter, it was unclear how the Greek Jews had gotten there, and as none of them spoke Polish, they couldn't explain their situation. It was known that they had all been sentenced to death, but in the turmoil of the last few months, the Germans were so preoccupied that they hadn't had the time to execute them.

Of course, it wouldn't have been Lala without a romantic touch. "The other day," she continued, "I was resting on a bench in front of the field hospital when a young Greek, looking very Middle Eastern, with intelligent sad black eyes sat next to me. He started to talk, trying to find a common language: first Spanish, then Italian, English, and finally French. We settled on French; I remembered a little from high school days. He introduced himself as Chaim Covo from Salonika, a former law student at the Sorbonne. We had hardly started talking when a Polish neighbor of Irka's called me aside and said, without hiding her disgust, 'Miss Halina, how can you talk to a dirty Jewish Greek prisoner? It's not becoming for a nice Polish girl!' "

Lala was shocked. "I thought the German occupation was over," she had retorted indignantly. "The woman looked at me with a mixture of surprise and contempt, spat on the ground, and walked away."

This incident had encouraged my sister to become friends with the young Greek "to prove to the Polish anti-Semites that I'm not afraid of them," as she put it. I knew Lala better. That wasn't her only motive. Such was her enthusiasm that she managed to convince Kazik to give his only suit to Chaim Covo, a true sacrifice in those days. Lala was sure of our victory; the letter ended with "See you in a few days."

It was already the end of the second week of fighting, and I didn't see anything to justify such optimism. Hospitals, schools, and churches were crowded with seriously wounded soldiers and civilians. Everything was in short supply: food, medicine, bandages, blood. Electricity had been cut off, and there was beginning to be a shortage of drinking water. Unofficial but reliable estimates placed the number of dead in the first two weeks at twenty thousand, and the wounded at three or four times that number. A major problem was finding space within the confines of the city to bury the dead.

The Allies continued to send supplies by air, but the German antiaircraft guns were in control of the skies, and the planes were forced to parachute the eagerly-awaited goods in from great heights. This resulted in weapons and provisions falling into German hands instead of ours. Seeing this was painful and frustrating. One night, when over a hundred planes, the highest number yet, arrived from the west, our hopes rose once more. But not for long: only fifteen parachutes landed in the part of the city occupied by the insurgents.

On the twentieth day of the uprising, I joined the Polish armed forces. I had decided that I didn't want to die hiding in a cellar. It seemed that such would be the fate of us all. The German bombings were getting more intense and the makeshift shelters no longer offered protection against the continued air assaults. If I had to die, I would die fighting. I hoped I'd be given a chance to kill at least one German before I was killed. It made no sense to sit and wait. I still remembered vividly the group of five Jews who had escaped with guns from the burning Warsaw Ghetto through Gibalski Street in the spring of 1943. Now it was time to join them.

I hadn't heard from Mother or from Lala since that first letter. I felt free to make my own decisions. Zosia didn't object. Fourteen was the youngest acceptable age for joining the resistance, so I didn't have to lie. They were rather surprised at the headquarters when I volunteered. There weren't many adolescents in the army. Because of the acute shortage of weapons and ammunition, I couldn't participate in the actual fighting. I was promised, however that if we received additional arms from the allies, I would be given a submachine gun, since a rifle might be too heavy for me. For the meantime, I was given a hand grenade and made a courier. I was assigned to deliver messages, supplies, ammunition, and food to outposts all over the inner city. This was a dangerous task because it entailed continuous exposure to the enemy, particularly snipers. The standard means of communication – radios and field telephones – were in very limited supply, so couriers were crucial to the war effort.

I didn't reveal my true identity. I was concerned about the possibility of being taken prisoner of war by the Germans, and I knew that I had a better chance for survival if they didn't know I was a Jew.

I was issued an ID card after a very emotional swearing-in ceremony. There were eight or nine of us new volunteers spanning the ages of fourteen to sixty. I was the youngest. The army lieutenant, obviously moved by my age, gave an impassioned speech about the bravery of Polish youth, unmatched among the nations of the world. In the background, a woman officer played Chopin's Revolutionary Etude, the unofficial anthem of the uprising. I was confused and couldn't understand why I was touched by his comments, or why I was crying. I was tempted to correct him, to tell him who I was, but I knew better.

I was proud to possess the ID card. It read "Armia Krajowa, district Warsaw, number 7868. This is to state that courier Julek Heybowicz (pseudonym) is a soldier of AK (Armia Krajowa): signed, District commander Col. Rajwan, Warsaw August 25, 1944."

The German bombing let up the week I joined the army. Instead of bombs, we were showered with leaflets calling for surrender. We gathered that the Germans were hurting and were eager to neutralize our impact on the war effort. The leaflets were masterpieces of perfidy. Signed by General Von Dem Bach, SS-Oberstugruppenführer, they read "Moved by human emotions, aware of my responsibility toward our common G-d, I declare a cease-fire between 6:00 and 8:00 a.m. to allow the good citizens of Warsaw to leave the city. I guarantee you life, work and bread. You know that the Bolsheviks are our only enemy. Leave Warsaw with white flags or handkerchiefs in your hands. This is a time-limited ultimatum."

We laughed at headquarters about the "human emotions" of an Oberstugruppenführer or, for that matter of any German. The few days of relative respite, however gave us an opportunity to reinforce the barricades and to concentrate on improving communication routes between outposts.

To avoid exposure to the enemy on open streets, we broke through walls between adjoining buildings, making it possible to cover long stretches without going out onto the street. We were like moles, digging a whole system of underground communications.

There were three other couriers in my unit: two boys, Stefan and Oleg, and a girl, Basia – all my age. From them, I found out why the lieutenant had been so moved during the swearing-in ceremony. The courier unit had originally been composed of five members. One of my predecessors had been killed the day before I joined, and his funeral had taken place just two hours before my induction into the army. He was buried in the yard. Through the window Stefan showed me a small grave, one of several, with a plain wooden cross on it. The other missing courier was in the hospital. He had stepped on a mine and had both his legs and his left arm blown off. The news about the dead boy didn't disturb me very much. Even seeing his grave at the doorstep was something I could cope with. I wasn't ready, however, for the second story. The possibility of being mutilated had never crossed my mind.

My two companions noticed my reaction – I must have grown very pale – but they didn't make fun of it. They were mature for their age, seasoned by the war. Basia even offered me a glass of water.

After a short lull, the fighting exploded with increased vehemence. I was active around the clock. Until I joined the army I hadn't been aware that, in this type of house-to-house warfare, one of a courier's major tasks was moving ammunition to outposts through endless trenches, cellars, and tunnels. The assignments were both dangerous and exhausting. In the third week of the uprising we were already producing our own ammunition, Molotov cocktails and flame throwers: primitive but effective weapons. As it was difficult to travel through the underground maze, only small quantities of ammunition could be carried at a time. The courier who had been killed had tried to shorten the trip by walking on the street. A sniper's bullet had hit one of the Molotov cocktails he was carrying, setting him afire. Occasionally a Molotov cocktail exploded on its own, making our work even more dangerous. We were forbidden to use open routes except when carrying messages of extreme urgency. We were also directed never, under any circumstances, to let the Germans catch us with a message. If there was no other way to avoid being caught, we had to use the hand grenade, our only weapon, to destroy ourselves and the message. I found this last order, which came as a directive from the commander-in-chief of the armed forces, General Bor-Komorowski, difficult to accept. It worried me. What if I didn't have the courage to pull the safety pin off the hand grenade when the moment came? Would I be endangering other people's lives if I surrendered with the secret information in my hand? For a brief moment I thought maybe I should resign, but I dismissed the thought rapidly, embarrassed that it had even crossed my mind. I had the feeling I would do the right thing when the time came.

7

Warsaw: The Bitter End

Toward the end of the third week of fighting, we had a new problem: the food shortage. With supplies depleted and stores empty, we had to look for alternative sources of food or, to be more exact, nourishment. We were cut off from the countryside. Fruit and produce were gone in a few days and meat by the end of the first week. We were fortunate in that, around the time the shortages became acute, the army conquered a midtown brewery, where we found an abundance of hops and a dozen heavy Belgian horses that had been used for delivery of beer. I ate horse meat with only slight hesitation; it was a little sweet but quite palatable. I only appreciated how good it was weeks later, when we started eating stray dogs and cats. Four weeks later, I didn't find mice and rats an improvement on cats and dogs. But by then it made no difference.

The hops were another problem. For a while, no one came up with a way to make them edible. Finally someone suggested soaking the hops overnight and then cooking them for several hours, turning them into a kind of porridge. Definitely edible, though of questionable taste. The main problem was the hops' hulls, which were indigestible and had to be spit out after each spoonful. The dish soon got a name, "Zupa pluj – spit soup." Fortunately, there was a huge supply of hops in the brewery. Trust the Poles when it comes to drinking!

Even the soup was not the worst thing. The real problem was the fat used to prepare our food. It was from a local shoe polish factory. Some people claimed it was wax, others said stearine or tallow. The optimists called it processed lard. It didn't really matter, the taste was neutral. But it was difficult to reconcile oneself to the idea of eating shoe polish.

Lala finally sent a second letter, less enthusiastic than her first. She was worried about being cut off from Mother and not having any information on her situation. She described her conversation with a senior Polish army officer. His assessment of our state of affairs was downright pessimistic. "We have to face the fact," Colonel Kujawa had said, "that only quick help from the outside can save the situation. This uprising is a romantic adventure, typical of the Polish way of thinking.

"Did you see our army?" he had asked rhetorically, "young boys in their twenties, proud, enthusiastic, and courageous. Dreamers! There are very few mature men among them. Our only solution is the Red Army. It is only twenty miles away, but we continue to antagonize the Russians, waiting for the allies from the west. A futile waiting. We are lost. We can't do it on our own."

The conversation must have had a devastating effect on my sister. From the smeared ink on the letter, I realized that she had been crying while writing. It was like a farewell letter to me. I burst out crying. I had never expected to survive Lala and Mother. Now I was completely alone!

Janek, the fourteen-year-old courier who had stepped on the mine, died of sepsis in the field hospital. He was buried in the courtyard of the headquarters, the seventh grave there. Four couriers, Stefan, Oleg, Basia, and I, were his pallbearers, and we lowered the small makeshift coffin into a shallow grave dug by one of the German war prisoners. Although I had never met Janek, I couldn't control my tears. Everyone, for that matter, was crying in silence. As was usual on such occasions, Lieutenant Janowski was playing Chopin's funeral march on the conference room piano. The music carried into the courtyard through the open window, the exploding bombs and machine-gun clatter offering a tragic counterpoint befitting the occasion. The priest was about to say the prayers over the open grave when a woman in her mid-thirties, dressed in worn-out army fatigues, came over to the clergyman and whispered something into his ear. She looked upset, her eyes swollen from crying. I heard someone say "that is Janek's mother." A short while later our commander, Captain Jarecki, joined the priest and the woman. I tried to catch what they were saying, but the piano music drowned out the conversation. A minute later the priest departed without saying a word, taking with him the small wooden cross with Janek's name on it. I suddenly realized that the dead boy I was helping to bury must have been a Jew in hiding like myself.

It took me a while to sort out my feelings. Grief, pride and fear followed each other in rapid succession. I tried not to show any of it, although my heart was beating a little faster than usual. I waited to see what would happen next. Captain Jarecki looked a little perturbed but didn't lose his usual composure. Turning to the group of soldiers and civilians gathered around the small grave, he started the eulogy: "Little Janek will not be buried in a religious ceremony," were his opening words. "We were just told by his mother that he was a Jew. It is a sad reflection on our society that even now, having been liberated from the Germans, he did not dare to reveal to us his true identity. Janek was the bravest boy I have ever met in my long years as a soldier. The Jewish people, and with them all the Poles, can be proud of this little boy. We were very privileged to have had him along with us."

This speech was too much for me, I was crying loudly, barely in control of my emotions, but grateful that no one was paying attention. The eulogy was unexpected, leaving everyone in a state of disbelief and confusion. Captain Jarecki stepped over to the coffin and alone shoveled all the dirt into the small grave.

Paradoxically, I could cope with this constant onslaught of painful and dangerous experiences at age fourteen not so much because of my strength but because of the very fact that events followed each other so rapidly. Before I could ponder one situation, I was wrestling with another. I was a juggler who had to be totally absorbed in his act. If I deflected my full attention, thought about the last ball instead of the next one, my act would be lost; I would have to leave the stage for good.

The day of Janek's funeral almost ended my life as well. We were preparing another offensive on the German YMCA near my mother's apartment house. As usual, the couriers were in charge of transferring some of the weapons and all the ammunition to the front lines. As a precaution in case one of us was caught and tortured by the Nazis for information, we were not told when the attack would start. But from the hectic pace of the preparations, I gathered that it would take place soon.

Late that night I was given another load of machine gun rounds to deliver from headquarters. I knew my way well. It was all underground, through interconnected cellars of adjacent buildings, except in a couple of places where the passage from one house to the next could not be made below street level, and walls were broken through on the second floor. The only problem at this point was the lack of light. We had had no electricity since the second week of the uprising, and my route was in total darkness. Flashlights were discouraged because a moving light makes an easy target, and I was forbidden to use a flashlight on the above-ground crossing, as it might reveal our communications route to the enemy.

I moved swiftly through the familiar path, using my tiny flashlight as sparingly as possible. I was close to exhaustion. It must have been the tenth time that day I was covering this route and I hoped that after this trip I would be able to go to sleep for a few hours at least. I started to climb the staircase of one of the above-ground crossings, now in total darkness, when I heard voices from the top of the staircase of the four-story building. I was surprised. I had met some people on my crossing before, but at night it was never more than one person, usually a courier going in the opposite direction. At first I thought it might be a wounded or dead soldier being transferred from the front lines. Puzzled and somewhat frightened by this unexpected development, I decided to stand still against the wall and wait for the people to pass me by. Seconds later the voices became clear, and I realized in horror that they were speaking German. It sounded like there were three or four men. They were only two floors above me, but I could not understand what they were saying. I couldn't figure out what had happened. Perhaps I'd become lost and in the darkness entered German territory? But that was impossible. I recognized the railing on the staircase. I had been here many times before. Could it be that the Germans were lost? Or maybe they were on some secret mission behind our lines? They obviously weren't attempting to conquer our outpost because there were only a few of them.

I had to act fast. My hand grenade was attached to my belt, but I easily convinced myself that, as I was not carrying any secret messages, I did not have to follow the commander-in-chief's orders not to get caught alive. To throw the grenade at the Germans was too frightening under the circumstances. I'd never done it before, and I was afraid it would explode in my face, the area was so restricted. The only alternative was to run back and warn headquarters about the invaders.

I set down the package of ammunition and started to walk back to the ground floor as quietly as possible, feeling the walls in the total darkness. The Germans, carrying large flashlights, began walking down the staircase much faster than I, unaware of my presence. Now I was sure they were lost. They spoke too loudly to be on a secret mission. In a minute or less they would catch up with me. I tried the door of the abandoned ground floor apartment; fortunately it was unlocked. I opened the door just enough to squeeze by, but it squeaked and I knew that the Germans had heard it. They stopped cold, turning off their flashlights.

I thought they were probably scared too. There was total silence, which added to the already unbearable tension. Once in the apartment, I dove into the hallway coat closet and stood there holding my breath, praying that the Germans had no dogs with them. Seconds later I heard them shout, "Wer ist da? – who is there?" As there was no answer, they must have dismissed the squeaking noise. They made their way cautiously to the cellar, probably into the next building.

In this respite from danger I had to plan my next step. I decided to proceed as rapidly as possible to my original goal, the outpost, now just two blocks away, and warn them of the German intrusion. I assumed that they would notify the headquarters through the field telephone. My only fear was that other German soldiers might be roaming the area. I left the ammunition where it was – carrying it would have slowed me down. I proceeded cautiously without using my flashlight.

They were worried about me at the outpost. I was behind schedule. After hearing what had happened, the lieutenant in charge immediately notified headquarters about the Germans. It was decided after a short consultation that while headquarters dispatched several men to round the Germans up, a unit from the outpost would set up an ambush for them in case they returned via the same route. I was to wait at the front until the situation was clear. I sat on the floor of the trench behind the barricades. Despite the noise of exploding artillery shells, I fell asleep instantly.

It was already dawn when I woke up. At first I wasn't sure where I was. After recognizing my location, I was terribly embarrassed not to have followed the important developments of last night. The commander of the unit greeted me with a big smile. Our ambush had worked beautifully. The Germans, realizing they were lost, had retraced their steps and had fallen into our trap half an hour after it was set up, in the building where I had first spotted them. All four – a major and three soldiers – were dead. We gained three automatic rifles, one submachine gun, and an apparently important document that was being deciphered at that moment in headquarters. The commander said that he had tried several times to wake me and tell me the good news, but to no avail. I would get up, salute, say "I'm at your orders, Commander," then turn around and go back to sleep in my corner. After his third attempt, with the whole unit watching my strange behavior, he had given up. He had checked with headquarters and discovered that I had been up for thirty-six hours.

The commander had more good news for me. In appreciation for my good judgment, which had led to the killing of the four Germans and the capture of badly needed weapons, I had been promoted to the rank of platoon leader in charge of the courier unit. I saluted him and went back to headquarters. This was another completely unexpected turn of events. Six hours earlier I had been seconds away from death; now I was returning to my unit a hero.

On my way back, I passed the bodies of the Germans on the staircase in the hallway of the building where I had encountered them the night before. The walls were splattered with blood. They were all very young, in their teens except for the officer. His head was split open, probably from a hand-grenade splinter, and something white was still oozing from the gaping hole. The others lay in puddles of blood. I stood there for several minutes, dumbfounded, almost in a trance. They were the first dead Germans I had seen, and it felt good to be at least partially responsible for their deaths.

The conquest of the German YMCA was probably the uprising's bloodiest battle in the inner city of Warsaw. It started at dawn and lasted nearly twenty-four hours. Although our losses were very high, the fighting having been decided in a face-to-face bayonet massacre, the victory was important because the Y was the last pocket of German resistance in our area.

Despite the spectacular conquest, the situation remained grave and at the same time absurd: At the end of the uprising's first month, both sides appeared to be scoring significant victories. The German army had recaptured several of Warsaw's suburbs and was closing in on the Old City. At the same time the inner city, the seat of the uprising's chief command, was getting rid of the remaining encircled Germans, solidifying defense lines, and bravely resisting the overwhelming superiority of the Nazi war machine. It seemed to me that even if the rest of Warsaw surrendered to the enemy, we would continue fighting until the bitter end.

With the strengthening of the German positions around Warsaw, the supplies from the Allies in the west came to a halt. Their air force could not break through the German anti-aircraft defense. The Soviets stubbornly continued their hands-off policy, probably waiting for us to surrender to their archenemy, another puzzling but not surprising development of this war.

Contrary to my expectation, the liberation of the YMCA did not reunite me with Mother. Her neighborhood was just three blocks away, but it was extremely dangerous, if not impossible, for anyone to go there.

It was in the German section of the city, and although we were both under the rule of the Armia Krajowa, the Germans had left behind many snipers on rooftops. For several days after the battle, I didn't know if Mother was alive. We had to wait until an underground communications system connected her street with the rest of the area. Four weeks into the fighting, my situation was as bad as ever and maybe even worse. I was tired, hungry, and alone.

Feeling desperate, not caring whether I lived or died, I volunteered for an assignment to bring supplies to the Old City, which was on the verge of surrender. If our mission succeeded I might at least be reunited with Lala. She had always been more inventive when it came to dealing with the Nazis, and I knew I needed her help. I was afraid of falling into German hands alone.

The man to lead our convoy, which consisted of ten volunteers, was the courier who had twice brought letters from Lala. He assured me that he knew where to find her. On several occasions he had visited the field hospital where she was a medic.

Some people in my unit thought that our mission was typical Polish bravado – impossible to execute. The Old City was completely cut off from the rest of Warsaw; the only way to get there was to walk through the sewer system, which allowed one to cross unnoticed under areas occupied by the enemy. The distance was a little more than two miles – four hours underground. Captain Komarek, the mission's leader, had covered the passage several times. But there were new complications at this point. The Germans had discovered our route and were watching it from above, through manholes in the area under their control. They did not dare descend into the sewer but listened attentively for sounds below. At the slightest suspicion of activity they would hurl a hand grenade down the manhole, killing everyone within a ten-foot radius. There were unconfirmed rumors that the enemy was planning to fill the system with poisonous gas, Yperite. According to experts, this made little sense; the gas would ascend to kill the Germans above ground as well. But in those last months of the war, the desperation was such that anything was possible.

Captain Komarek looked and acted like the model Polish officer. Tall and blue-eyed, his blond hair bordering on white, he (unlike most of us) wore a clean, perfectly pressed Polish cavalry uniform, circa 1939. The outfit was complemented by a pair of riding boots, shined to perfection. Was he using the same polishing wax we were eating with our hops?

Talking to me he referred to Lala knowingly as "your sister, the medic Judita." (Judita was the nickname Lala had been given in her army unit after someone had commented on her Semitic appearance.)

The group of volunteers was a mixed bag of hotheads, true patriots, and people who, like myself, wanted to get into the Old City. There was one boy my age and one woman. We all carried ammunition. I was given a knapsack full of Molotov cocktails made in our makeshift weapons workshop. After taking on this cargo I began to have second thoughts about the wisdom of joining the group. The thought of having a load of easily triggered homemade explosives on my back made me acutely anxious. A sudden jump, a fall or a slip, could mean catastrophe. It was too late to change my mind, though. The spirits of the others were high, and no one even mentioned danger. They were discussing the contents of the sludge we were about to walk in – gallows humor, I guess.

Captain Komarek's speech was short and unemotional. He talked while we were changing our shoes for high rubber boots; the sewage was up to one's knees in some areas. He knew the route very well, he said. It should take us exactly three hours and twenty minutes. Describing the Germans as "stupid Krauts," he claimed that they were more afraid than we were. He also had a plan to outwit them: Before we reached each manhole, we would hurl a stone into the sewage. Hearing a splash, the Germans would assume we were passing by and throw a hand grenade down. Seconds after the explosion, we would pass rapidly under the open manhole.

I knew from my experience with other Polish officers that the anticipation of military events always sounded better than their reality. Such descriptions almost followed a formula: the enemy is dumb. We outwit him and show our legendary courage. Most of us get killed, but we prevail. Our dead are buried with the highest military honors. My father used to describe stories like this in Yiddish as "bobbe-myseh – grandma's tales." Although I could not imagine any of my ancestors telling tall tales of heroism, I suspected that the captain's plan had some of the unrealistic qualities my father was referring to. For instance, I wanted to know what would happen if the Germans threw in two hand grenades, one after another. How would we know when to move ahead? But no one was asking questions. We were each handed a pint of vodka – the rarest and most desirable of all possessions at this point in the uprising. The captain hesitated for a second before giving me the small bottle, but then he said, "you should have it too: you are a man, one of us." We were to use it only in "dire emergencies" – whatever that meant! We were ready to go.

It was 10 p.m. when we started to descend the slippery iron footholes of a manhole. I was third from the end. It was a beautiful starlit night, in sharp contrast to what awaited us underground. The sewage pipe was relatively large where we entered, almost five feet in diameter. It was perfect for me, but the captain and some of the men had to bend a little. The sludge was only ankle deep, but the air was vile; it reeked of decayed debris, ammonia, garbage, and human excrement. We proceeded cautiously, the captain leading. It was pitch dark. We all had flashlights, but we were to use them only in extreme need, as batteries were rare and precious. Also, their light would make us visible from above. After about thirty minutes of uneventful plodding through the thick sludge, we encountered two men marching in the opposite direction. They looked frightening in the dim light of our flashlights. Their faces were encrusted with sludge, which gave them a strange, mummified appearance. Their story was not coherent. They claimed to have been lost, to have walked in the sewer for the last twelve hours unable to find their destination. Captain Komarek wanted to tell them how to proceed, but they moved on without listening and disappeared into the darkness of the cavernous system. Someone commented that they might have been intoxicated by the fumes and the ammonia from the decaying matter. That happened to people who were underground much longer than six hours.

The sludge got deeper, to midcalf, and it was very slippery. I was afraid that I might fall and explode one of the Molotov cocktails. I tried to hold on to the rounded wall, but it was slippery too and offered limited support. To make things worse, the pipes were getting progressively narrower. By now I had to bend in order to walk without hitting my head. The tall men in the unit were bent double, some on their knees, carrying their heavy loads in front of them.

We almost failed to see the first open manhole in German-occupied territory. Walking at night offered some protection, as the Germans couldn't see us from above, but it also had the disadvantage of making it difficult to discern which manholes were open and which were not. Fortunately, the man leading our outfit (the captain was in the back helping the other fourteen-year-old, who had suddenly started to cry) saw a reflection of a star in the thick sludge and realized that it was from an open manhole. We froze, almost falling over one another. After retreating several yards, Captain Komarek followed the master plan. He threw an object into the sludge just under the cover and it made a loud splash. We heard voices from the street, and then there was a frighteningly loud explosion that blew us off our feet into the cold, muddy, filthy water. It must have been more than a hand grenade. The captain's next command came in a whisper, "move quickly past the manhole."

We proceeded in silence now, some of us on all fours. My heart was thumping rapidly. I could hardly catch my breath, waiting for the Germans to throw in the second grenade. They didn't. Instead, we heard an announcement in Polish, through a bullhorn, calling on us to surrender, assuring us that we would be treated according to the Geneva Convention. Such offers were traps. The Germans machine-gunned people the moment they emerged from the manhole.

We rested, trying to recover from the events of the last few minutes. Everyone was silent except the other boy whose sobbing had become uncontrollable. The captain was trying to reassure him without success. All but inaudibly, interrupted by sobs, the boy was saying "I want to go back, I want my mother." Hesitantly, the captain decided to let him go. Each of us took an additional Molotov cocktail from the boy's knapsack, and he started on his way. Captain Komarek looked at me. He didn't ask anything and I didn't say a word. I was determined to continue. Minutes later we heard a loud explosion and blood-curdling scream. It was the boy, probably killed by a German hand grenade as he passed under the manhole we had just slipped by.

Our leader must have realized that the Germans would not stop with the first hand grenade, for he gave up his strategy of outwitting the "stupid Krauts." By the time we approached the next open manhole, our new orders were to walk slowly, in complete silence. It worked; they didn't notice us.

Now we were faced with a new problem: the sludge was getting thicker and deeper, reaching my waist. My shortness, an advantage in the earlier tunnel, was now a serious handicap. Someone suggested that the Germans were trying to drown us in excrement by setting up a dam in the section under their control. This must have been on everybody's mind. Once verbalized, it somehow changed from a personal fear to a potential reality. Silence followed the remark. I assumed that everyone was feeling the same way, gripped by the fear of a horrible death, drowning in sewage. Being the shortest in the group, I thought of myself as the most vulnerable, but I cared less and less as time went by. I must have been getting intoxicated by the fumes.

By the time we approached the third manhole, the situation had reached crisis proportions. Two of the men, both in their early twenties, announced that they had had enough; they couldn't take it anymore. They wanted to surrender to the Germans.

The captain tried at first to dissuade them, calling their decision "insane, suicidal." They would not relent. Then he threatened to shoot them for disobedience, for treason. As might have been expected, they didn't care, and challenged him to go ahead. There was no way to stop them. One of the men took off his shirt, which must have been white at some point, and made a makeshift flag, using his arm as the flagpole. We all focused our flashlights on him, trying to help in his preparation for the climb to the surface. He and his colleague handed their guns to Captain Komarek, who in turn, gave one to me and the other to the woman. We were the only ones who hadn't carried guns before.

The man with the white flag didn't say goodbye. Instead, he said "Long Live Poland!" a farewell I always associated with people about to be executed. He walked cautiously, the few steps that separated us from the manhole, followed closely by his companion, who was holding onto him. They didn't use flashlights to avoid being detected before their climb. It was a pathetic sight, two seasoned soldiers walking like helpless frightened children, each waving a white rag.

The man with the flag started to climb, his arm stretched above him. There was total silence until he was halfway out and then, suddenly, a short burst of machine-gun fire. I didn't hear his scream; his head was above the ground. His body fell with a splash into the sewer, dragging in the second man, who sank to the bottom under the weight of the dead body. The captain motioned us to retreat. He was right this time. The Germans followed the shooting with a hand grenade, blowing both men to pieces. We waited a few minutes and then continued in the bloody sludge, managing to pass under the manhole undetected. There were only seven of us out of the original ten. We were supposedly one hour away from our destination.

We didn't make it. The sewage was getting steadily deeper. It was up to my chest when Captain Komarek ordered the retreat. He told us to drop the ammunition we were carrying, in order to make the trip back easier. I was by then totally exhausted, and had no doubt that if we hadn't gone back, I would have drowned.

Zosia shrieked with fright when she saw me back at home covered with dried sludge. I had no strength to answer her questions. I literally had to be carried by the captain and another man for the last stretch underground. I fell into a deep sleep from which I woke delirious forty-eight hours later. I had a 104-degree fever caused by a severe ear infection caused by the putrid sewage. At first I thought I was hallucinating: I saw my mother sitting next to me, applying cold compresses to my burning forehead. Only when I heard her voice did I realize that she was in fact with me. I was happy, overwhelmed, but could not utter a word. She noticed by the way I looked at her that I had recognized her, and then her beautiful blue eyes became cloudy.

I was very sick for over a week. There was serious doubt that I would pull through. After a great deal of pleading, a doctor came to see me. All physicians were working round the clock in the field hospitals caring for the wounded; no one made house calls unless a patient was critically ill. The doctor was no help. There was no medication available. He diagnosed an inner-ear infection and told Mother that due to severe malnutrition my resistance was low; the prognosis was poor. She later told me that he hadn't had much hope for me.

Typically, Mother remained unperturbed by the doctor's grim statement and continued to take care of me day and night. From Rockschmidt's apartment she brought me two bottles of raspberry syrup and kept forcing me to drink endless glasses of water with this elixir. Our family had always ascribed special magical curative powers to raspberry syrup. Before the war we would have it homemade, prepared by some of my father's poor relatives who lived in the country and picked the berries themselves. In the early fall, one of the country cousins would come by train bringing a large wicker basket full of preserves and syrup for which my father would pay him generously. The syrup must have symbolized the elusive connection with the wholesome earth that both my mother and my father had longed for since their early childhood.

The raspberry treatment worked once more. Although very weak, I was on my feet eight days after my misbegotten adventure to the Old City. It was also the day when the Old City fell into German Hands.

We were very worried about what the Germans might do to Lala. We hoped that she had left the field hospital where she was known as Judita before the Nazis took over. There were reports that the German army was vicious to the surrendering insurgents, killing all the wounded.

Mother did not discuss it, but I could see she was worried about Lala. Mother had changed a great deal during the month we had been separated. She had lost weight; her face looked drawn; her hair was starting to gray. For the first time she looked older than forty. She didn't speak unless questioned. Her interaction with people was minimal.

Zosia told me later that when Mother had arrived, the night I left for the Old City, she had looked strange, forlorn and frightened, consumed with anguish. Her only question was "where are my children?" Upon hearing the answer, she had started to cry and then gone to sleep. She had remained in a trance-like state until my return. I recalled Mother's earlier reaction to the belief that Lala had been captured, when we still lived in Swoszowice, and her wish to commit suicide then. Now I anxiously watched her behavior. Even in the early days I had been worried that my mother might commit suicide.

Way back in 1940, when we had been under Russian occupation and my father had gone into hiding every night, I was wakened one morning by a blood-curdling, high-pitched shriek that I recognized as Mother's. I ran into my parents' bedroom; the bed was empty, my mother gone. I leaped toward the entrance door, which I found ajar. Outside I found Mother leaning over the staircase railing shouting "Help! Help!" I bent over the railing and looked three flights down to the bottom of the secular staircase; there the bleeding body of a woman was lying motionless. When Mother calmed down, she told us what had happened. At about eight o'clock she left to go shopping. As she opened the door to the staircase (we had no elevator), she had noticed a woman leaning with half of her body over the railing. It was clear that the woman was about to jump. Mother screamed and tried to grab her, but it was too late. The woman flung herself over and, seconds later, was lying on the marble floor at the bottom of the staircase, her brain oozing from a smashed skull.

Worried in those days about my parents, I had associated the scream with Mother and thought it was she who had jumped. It was something I had never forgotten. Now I didn't let Mother leave my sight. We tried to get information about the fate of the surrendering population; but with the electricity gone there were no radios except for a transmitter in headquarters, and we had no way of knowing what was happening.

Lala arrived at Zosia's the night the Old City fell. She had been in the last group of soldiers to escape through the sewers. She was tired and covered with sludge, but in good spirits, happy to be with us again.

The story of how she managed to join this group was the ultimate in ingenuity and manipulation, the crowning glory of her four-year career as an escape and survival artist. She had given each of the commanding officers a different reason why they should take her along. Some of her arguments were true, such as the fact that she was Jewish; other stories, claiming that her grandfather was the Polish ambassador to England, or promising to marry the officer immediately after the war, were a figment of her imagination, her ability to tell anyone whatever was wanted or expected from her convincingly. Once more, it was Lala at her best, displaying the talent that helped us all survive.

All of us, Zosia, Marysia, and I, were excited to be with Lala. Luck seemed to be on our side, or was it ingenuity? But Mother reacted strangely to Lala's return. Speechless, she just embraced my sister and cried silently. I sensed that she was barely coping with all this. The last series of frightening events, just when we were about to be liberated, was more than she could bear.

Returning to my unit after an absence of nearly two weeks, I found everyone in low spirits, without hope. There was little fighting going on in the sixth week of the uprising. Our commander was negotiating a surrender with General Von Dem Bach, the chief of the German armed forces in Warsaw. We were ready to give up the fighting if the Germans would agree to treat us according to the Geneva Convention, without retaliatory punishment and with full POW privileges for the participants of the uprising. The Germans were eager to finish the Warsaw involvement but still too conceited to give us our rights. We chose to continue fighting. The situation was grim. There was almost no food, no medical supplies. There were vast numbers of wounded, and no space to bury the dead: only water, from the wells that had been dug since the uprising, was in good supply. It seemed the world had forgotten us completely. There were no more planes from the Allies. Our batteries were too weak to maintain regular radio contacts with London, and there was almost no contact with the Russians, although the latter were geographically closer, having conquered the suburb of Praga, just across the Vistula.

In the sixth week, the Soviet general Rokossovski sent a courier to General Bor-Komorowski, our commander-in-chief, with a request to coordinate our strategy with that of the Russian army. The Poles reluctantly agreed to cooperate. It had taken forty days of furious fighting, and close to a hundred thousand casualties, for us to be willing to compromise with the Russians. It was too late, though. The Soviet army wasn't ready to attack immediately, and we weren't able to wait much longer. Now we were too weak and too hungry to resist the Germans. As an expression of good will, the Russians offered to send some food. The following day a plane appeared in the skies and, flying low, began dropping bags of food into the inner city. We watched in disbelief. The bags had no parachutes!

We would have laughed if it hadn't been so tragic. A sack with a hundred pounds of kasha fell on Zosia's apartment house. It went through the roof and the third-story ceiling and floor, and landed on the second floor, killing a canary. All those nights we spent in the cellar thinking we were safe – and a bag of kasha almost demolished the house! To get killed, after five years of superhuman efforts, by a sack of groats!

We had all developed individual styles of dealing with peril. Marysia, for example, would rapidly shift from one activity to another, so she was too busy to be aware of her surroundings. One day she returned home from one of her many volunteer jobs struggling to catch her breath. "You wouldn't believe what happened," she said when I opened the door. "A bomb exploded two feet away from me just as I was about to leave the hospital. I thought I would drop dead from fear!" That was Marysia: oblivious to real danger, frightened by the idea rather than the event.

My last brush with death during the uprising came courtesy of Captain Komarek, the leader of that unfortunate walk in the sewer. He appeared unexpectedly one day in headquarters and told my commander that he had to get to the front lines in our district on an important assignment, and needed a courier to show him the way. Spotting me, he asked whether I would guide him to his destination.

After receiving the required approval, we left on our mission. It wasn't far, three or four blocks maybe, but it would take at least fifteen minutes to get through the maze of underground tunnels and cellars. Having recovered from the sewer escapade a long time ago, Captain Komarek was his usual dapper and courageous self. It was hard to believe how impeccably dressed he was in the eighth week of the uprising. He was happy to see me. You are a tough, Platoon Leader Julek," he said. He was the first to address me by my official title. "I was pleased with your performance in the sewer. That other kid was a mama's boy. We would have outwitted the dumb Krauts if not for the stupid sewage." It was obvious that he hadn't learned his lesson; the Germans weren't dumb, they were vicious murderers lying in wait.

After crossing two cellars, the captain addressed me again. "We are wasting precious time, Platoon Leader Julek. I could be telling our boys on the front line how to kill more Krauts. What shortcut can we take?" The way to save time was to walk on the streets in full view of the enemy. I was surprised that he would ask such a question. Did he want to risk our lives again? Carried away by his compliments, I told him of the alternate route. "You are not afraid to go this way, are you?" asked Captain Komarek.

I had no choice. We ascended the cellar staircase and tried the door leading to the street. It was locked. No one had used this door in close to eight weeks. The captain retreated several steps and then charged the glass door, kicking it open with his polished riding boot. With the door shattered, we proceeded to the street. I was leading. It was the first time since the uprising began that I was on the street in this neighborhood. It was frightening to be in the abandoned above-ground world. The streets were covered with debris: broken glass, plaster, bricks, and mortar. The carcass of a dead horse, half rotten and half dried out, lay in the street, its cart overturned. A burned trolley and a few burned-out cars completed the eerie picture. It was quiet: just an occasional burst of machine-gun fire in the distance. We had to walk carefully so as not to trip over mounds of glass.

We turned the corner and headed swiftly across the street, probably in full view of the enemy, although I wasn't sure. I didn't dare look around. We just darted to the other side and pressed ourselves against the wall, creating the smallest possible target in case they did see us. But everything was quiet. The captain looked at me triumphantly. He had been right again. We were now less than two hundred feet from our goal. One more street crossing and we would be there. We could see the building we were headed for from where we stood. It was a lovely two-story Victorian town house, separated from the street by a large garden, now overgrown. A heavy, ornate iron fence, with a narrow gate on the right, separated the property from the street. Captain Komarek crossed first. He was in such a hurry he almost tripped over the remains of a dead dog that was lying on the pavement. I followed seconds later.

We were both at the gate. I grasped the handle and tried to open the door. It was locked. We were stuck. I looked angrily at the captain. Suddenly a shot rang out: a bullet hit the gate five or six inches above my head. I felt very faint, but the captain didn't lose his composure. "Those stupid Krauts!" he said. "They don't even know how to aim."

This man must be insane, I thought. How did I get myself into this situation? Now we were ringing the bell, unaware that, because of the lack of electricity, it wasn't functioning.

The second and third shots were aimed at my companion. Both missed him by some three or four inches. "His aim is hopeless," was the next quip.

We knew now that a sniper had spotted us. We were at a loss as to what to do. Going back made no sense: we would be equally exposed. I was paralyzed with fear and rage. The next bullet hit, less than two inches above my head. I felt a fine dust of paint and iron falling on my hair.

"I have to admit he's getting better," the captain commented. He seemed truly oblivious to the danger.

I felt the urge to run. How could I just stand there, a living target? Fortunately, the soldiers in the town house noticed us, and one of them rushed to the gate to open it. There were two more shots before the door was thrown open, but they missed.

The commander of the unit reprimanded us for taking unnecessary risks, but Captain Komarek explained that he was new to the area and had just followed my suggestions.

In the last week of the uprising there was not more fighting: there had been an undeclared cease-fire. We knew we had lost. All the suburbs had fallen to the Germans by then. Now the question was of negotiating the conditions of surrender. On October 2, 1944, General Bor-Komorowski, the commander-in-chief of the uprising, surrendered the inner city to the general of the SS, Oberstugruppenführer Von Dem Bach. Sixty-three days of fighting had left us weak, demoralized, and hungry. Close to two hundred thousand people- one in six- had lost their lives in vain.

With the signing of the official surrender, the Poles had that feeling of military pride they always seemed so eager to fight for. Ironically, that honor was being bestowed on them by their archenemies, the Germans. The agreement called for full prisoner-of-war rights according to the Geneva Convention for all members of the fighting Armia Krajow. The rest of the population was to be divided into two groups: those who could work and would be sent as slave labor to Germany, and those too old or too young to work, who could stay in Poland in places of their choice, without being detained.

Once the conditions of our capitulation were made public, we sat down with Zosia and Marysia to discuss our options. Lala, Marysia, and I were eligible for prisoner-of-war camp. Mother and Zosia, both in their early forties would probably have a choice between staying in Poland or going to Germany. The Nazis didn't usually deport people over thirty-five, fearing that they would not work hard enough.

Obviously, all those choices were predicated on our ability to maintain a Christian identity. Lala was concerned that I wouldn't be able to survive the harsh atmosphere of a Polish stalag on my own. Mother thought that it would be risky for Lala and Marysia to become

POWs as there had been no women in those camps until now. They would be vulnerable to Germans and Poles alike. Marysia started to giggle at Mother's comments, which helped us to decide against the POW strategy. What was left, though, was the choice between staying somewhere around Warsaw to wait for the next Russian offensive, probably within a few months, or going to Germany. Lala argued that we would be safer in Germany, lost in the refugee crowd, as in Poland we might be discovered as Jews and sent to Auschwitz, even this late in the war. Although I concurred with Lala, I was very unhappy with this conclusion. It meant probably another long year until we would be liberated, until this war would be over. We would be in the heartland of Germany, and there was no doubt in our minds that the Nazis would fight to the bitter end.

8

Hell Revisited

P acking our belongings was more than painful. We were all sapped of all energy: the idea of starting from scratch after four years of nightmarish escapades was difficult to accept.

It was a chilly October day when we walked out of Warsaw with thousands of other refugees. We certainly looked different than we did on our first trip, in September 1939. Mother was wearing Mrs. Rockschmidt's winter coat with a silver fox collar and Mr. Rockschmidt's hat, as this was the only one available. She had a small knapsack on her back overflowing with personal belongings. In her hands were a shopping bag and a man's umbrella. Lala wore an orange woolen skirt, a green sweater, and a pin striped man's jacket. Our biggest problem was finding appropriate clothes for me, as I had worn an army uniform all through the uprising, and shorts before that. Mother shortened the pants that came with Lala's jacket. Having been made for a very tall man, they looked like a floor-length skirt on me, but I had no choice. I wore a shirt and Marysia's red pullover. I had no coat. I had lost a lot of weight during the uprising, and the combination of sunken cheeks, strange-looking clothes, and dirty, matted hair made me look closer to a scarecrow than a soldier. I had become very sensitive to my appearance since the beginning of my Aryan life and at first the new image made me feel vulnerable. But I looked around and was immediately reassured. This was a pathetic-looking crowd. A bunch of sad, haggard, undernourished refugees, barely making it on that march into a new exile. For the first time since the war began I felt I belonged.

As Mother had our only knapsack, we had to wrap the rest of our belongings in a white sheet and make a bundle of it. Threading the bundle on a broomstick and placing the ends on our shoulders, we set out, Lala leading. We had to walk almost fifteen miles to a town called Pruszków, where the Germans had set up a temporary detention camp in the hangars of a former airplane factory. From there we were to be sent to our final destination, a labor camp in Germany.

This march took us close to seven hours. We walked in columns, twenty to thirty abreast, humiliated and except for the occasional cry of a baby or child, silent. Everyone around us looked exhausted, haggard, and severely undernourished. We walked with our heads down, our eyes glued to the road, trying to ignore the German soldiers guarding the column. Units of the insurgent army were walking separately from the civilians, having surrendered their weapons to the victors. The enemy soldiers were lined up along the road, one about every two hundred feet. They were not belligerent. I seemed to detect sympathy in some of them. What they were witnessing was probably astonishing even to seasoned murderers. It must have been the first time in modern history that a capital city of almost a million people-a vast metropolis- would be completely abandoned.

It started to rain, and Mother tried to get us under her umbrella, but that wasn't possible because of the way Lala and I had to carry our bundle on the stick. We elected to have our belongings, rather than ourselves, protected from the rain. And so we walked: Lala, then Mother, her umbrella covering the makeshift package, then me. Our march seemed interminable.

Once the city was behind us, we found the residents of Warsaw's distant suburbs lining the road along with the German soldiers. Many were crying, watching the pathetic, slow moving column. Some were handing out food, the first fruits and vegetables we had seen in two months. Mother, Lala, and I were nervously reviewing our plans. The sight of the German soldiers with their submachine guns had a greater impact than we had expected. After having been free and able to fight them, being once more at their mercy made us extremely anxious. Hell revisited. Again I was worried about looking Jewish now that I had lost so much weight. Mother's depressed appearance was very disconcerting. I knew we couldn't rely on her anymore. It seemed that I had the additional burden of protecting her.

As soon as the rain stopped, we were aware of a new danger. The army was replaced by Gestapo units, which looked much more menacing. Some of them made obscene remarks whenever young women walked by and had, on a few occasions, yanked women from the column. Lala put on an old kerchief and we stuffed a towel under her shirt to create the appearance of a hunchback.

A few kilometers from Pruszków a man in our column announced loudly and happily, "they just caught three Jew boys in a group ahead of us! I hope they catch them all! I saw lots of Jews crawl out of hiding during the uprising." We just looked at each other and, without a word moved cautiously toward the center of the slow-moving column. We knew we were right to go to Germany: it was definitely unsafe here among the Poles.

How to describe Pruszków? The vast hangars of the former airplane factory were turned into a Durchgangslager, a transition camp. Each of the arriving refugees was given a small area of filthy, oil-soaked cement floor to spread his belongings. The Germans had surrounded the plant with a barbed-wire fence that was easy to penetrate. It divided the area into two sections: one for new arrivals, and one for people selected for slave labor in Germany. At first we were all directed toward the general area. Even the efficient Germans had difficulty coping with the thousands of refugees; it would probably be days before we were processed. Red Cross officials stood by impotently watching our misery, helping no one. They were all smiling but unapproachable; Swiss, clean, and impeccably dressed. Their presence gave the Nazis the air of respectability they were eager to achieve now, so close to the end of the war. To us it was another sign of having been left, ignored, abandoned by the world.

Filth, lice, bedbugs, and the lack of even minimal hygienic facilities made our existence in Pruszków intolerable. The five of us huddled in the assigned area. Lala and Marysia occasionally left to find out what was happening and try to buy some additional food to supplement the watery turnip soup we were given twice a day. After forty-eight hours, we were told to proceed to the registration area. To ensure our being sent to Germany together, Mother and Zosia slipped into Lala's and Marysia's dresses, which helped them look younger. Heavily applied lipstick and rouge also made Mother appear younger, if somewhat cheap and vulgar.

As it turned out, we need not have worried. At this point the Germans needed every able-bodied person they could find. All Germans from sixteen to sixty-five had been mobilized. Factories and farms were entirely dependent on slave labor. We were moved to the section reserved for those going to Germany. We were deloused with a chemical spray and – six hours later – loaded on a freight train to be transported to an unknown destination.

Moving into an uncharted new territory full of unfamiliar risks and unpredictable dangers, we were capitalizing on the notion that the

Germans were incapable of distinguishing Polish Jews from Polish Christians, while Poles could easily pick up the nuances of our different upbringings. Naively, we were trusting the Germans to take us to labor camps not to the extermination camps. But why should we trust them, climbing into the overcrowded cattle car, the type I had seen years ago on my way from Swoszowice to Warsaw? I vividly remember the panic-ridden voices of those Jews bound for the death camps, crying, "Where are they taking us?" The wall of silence these questions had met became suddenly poignant. Where am I going?

Fortunately, we found a corner place on the floor of the car not far from the narrow, slot-like window. It offered a little privacy. Lala counted sixty people once the door was closed. It was very crowded. Knowing the distance between Warsaw and central Germany, we estimated that the trip would take at least thirty-six hours and much longer if we were being sent to the northern or western part of the country. I didn't share any of my concerns with Mother or Lala, fearing to upset them even more.

The door on our car was closed but not locked. This boded well. The narrow window was open – just two loosely strung barbed wires across it. This also was encouraging. As far as I could recall, the windows on the train bound for Auschwitz had bars, thick bars. I asked Lala to lift me to the window, which was about a foot under the car roof, and I looked out. Only two or three German soldiers were guarding the train. They sat casually on the stairs in front of the railroad station, their semiautomatic rifles on the floor. It looked safe. We were being treated as volunteers, which in some absurd sense we were, and not as prisoners.

Most of the passengers in our car were young women. The men must have opted for the POW camps. There were several couples and one family with two teenage boys.

The door opened. Red Cross inspection and food: half a pound of black bread and a turnip for each one of us. The fat, balding Swiss official expressed his approval of our condition to the German officer that accompanied him. The door was closed. I heard an iron bar being pushed on the outside. We were locked in. My assessment had been wrong.

The train pulled out of the station about an hour later. Within minutes the rhythmic sound of the wheels lulled me to sleep. I woke up suddenly in total darkness, hearing a woman shriek. It took me a while to orient myself. Someone lit a match. In the far corner of the car a young woman was screaming at the top of her lungs, "Lice! Lice! Lice! I can't take it anymore. I want out, let me out!"

Two women grabbed her arms, wrestling her down to the floor. A man lit a candle. Everybody was awake now. The young woman freed herself from those trying to restrain her, dashed toward the locked door of the speeding train, trampling anyone in her way. Her body was covered with deep scratches, some oozing blood. It was a frightening sight. She pulled at the heavy door of the speeding train. A man tried to stop her, but she shook him off like a fly. Her insanity had given her superhuman strength. Two other men crept toward her. They must have been planning the move: one of them grabbed her from behind in a half nelson while the other struck her in the face with his fist. She fell unconscious, blood gushing from her nose. The men tied her arms and legs with a rope. The light went out. No one said a word. I looked at my watch: it was three in the morning. I snuggled against my mother but I couldn't sleep. I kept wondering whether the lice could do that to anyone or whether this woman was crazy. I kept seeing her blood-covered body for the rest of the night.

Around six o'clock the train came to a halt. It was already dawn. The doors were opened. We were in a small, seemingly abandoned railroad station. The guards let us out. We asked a German soldier where we were but he didn't answer.

They carried the madwoman out, her arms and legs still tied. Now she was pleading for help, obviously frightened of the armed soldiers. Someone speculated that they would execute her on the spot (the Nazis exterminated all mentally ill patients), but we had no way of finding out. I doubt anyone really cared at this point. For us it meant one less person on the overcrowded train. We were given lukewarm broth, basically water with slices of beets floating in it, and a piece of bread. The door was locked again.

It was a very long day that followed the morning stop. Although already October, it was unbearably hot in the all-but-sealed car. The stench of sweat made the heat more unbearable. The train didn't stop for the next twelve hours. There was total silence. Most of us were half-asleep or semiconscious.

Early in the afternoon a near knife brawl between two drunken men broke the silence. They were threatening each other, the issue being a young girl who was sitting between them. The man who had knocked out the screaming woman the night before demanded that they turn in their pocket knives. They did so meekly, without resistance. He was obviously becoming the leader of the group.

When they opened the door the next time even the Germans were surprised to see our condition. A lot of screaming in German followed, after which we were allowed to leave the train for over an hour. An older woman sitting near Zosia who had seemed to be dozing turned out to have died in her sleep, probably of heat prostration. The Germans carried the body out and left it in a field beside the tracks when the train pulled away. The woman's daughter and teenage granddaughter sobbed uncontrollably for the rest of the journey, adding to the already tense atmosphere. We were given the same soup but a double portion of bread. The German officer in charge of the train announced over the bullhorn that from now on there would be more frequent stops and the doors would be left open to improve the ventilation. These announcements lifted our spirits. The promises, minimal as they were, indicated at least some degree of concern for our welfare.

That night we were exposed to the reverse of the day's experiences: unbearable cold. The overcrowding suddenly became an asset. We all huddled as close as possible to conserve the heat.

The 6 a.m. stop was made in Germany. We pulled onto the side tracks of a relatively large but obscure railroad station. The guards led us to the public toilets in groups of twenty. German civilians and military personnel regarded us with a mixture of pity and disgust. I understood from their reactions when I saw myself in the mirror above the immaculately clean sink: I was emaciated and filthy. My sunken cheeks and the black rings under my eyes completed the picture. What a sight! I wasn't troubled by this, however. Once again I felt capable of tuning in to what went on around me and effectively taking control of the situation. I had learned a lot about survival over the past five years.

There were rumors on the train, supposedly based on information from one of the guards that unless there were unforeseen delays due to heavy railroad schedules, we would be arriving that night in Wilhelmshagen, a labor camp near Berlin. It was welcome news. By nighttime we would have been on the train close to forty hours.

I sat near Lala, and we started to plan our strategy once we got into camp. Mother was dozing off. Zosia and Marysia were playing cards with a third woman, and we chose not to disturb them. Lala was now treating me as an adult; I was five months short of being fifteen. We knew that the responsibility for the five of us lay on both our shoulders. I enjoyed our conversations. They were not always limited to practical issues, but often related to our feelings about the war, the Germans as people, and ourselves. For the first time we began to question the worth of fighting so hard for survival. It was Lala's contention that when the war was over the Germans would be damned forever by the peoples of the world for what they had done to millions of innocent victims. Even if they managed to rebuild their destroyed country, they would never recover from the moral decay that would follow Hitler's demise. "A nation of murderers," she would say, "cannot survive in the civilized world. Its crimes have to corrode its very matrix." Whether she was right or was just expressing a wishful fantasy, I liked to listen to her. I was at home with this kind of thinking. It reminded me of my father's quoting Sir Anthony Eden, the British foreign secretary, who had said sometime early in the war, "we shall win, you know, because ours are decent, democratic societies with the ultimate moral resources that win wars. It will be a long, brutal war. But we'll win in the end." I found the idea of historical justice very soothing.

Our plans hinged on whether the Germans intended to keep us in the labor camp or to disperse us to local factories and farms. In the latter case, we would try to contact Rockschmidt, whose estate was in Erzberg, some forty miles east of Berlin. We knew that he had almost forty foreign slave laborers employed on his seven-hundred-acre ranch, and we hoped he'd be willing to take three or five more. It wouldn't cost him anything, since the Germans didn't pay captive laborers. The main problem would be getting in touch with him.

We got to Wilhelmshagen earlier than predicted, around seven in the evening. The train stopped in a wooded area. We were told to march in columns of six, carrying our belongings, toward a camp that was not more than half a mile away. From where our train halted, we could see the camp's high watchtowers, with machine guns and gigantic reflectors facing all directions. The presence of the towers was alarming; I associated them with concentration camps, not labor camps. Why was there such an elaborate system to guard volunteer workers?

I looked around anxiously to see whether there were any high smokestacks from crematoria, but there were none in sight. I was suspicious. I wanted to share my thoughts with Lala. Maybe we should still try to run away. It wouldn't be difficult to hide in the woods around the train, but I saw that she was preoccupied, and I didn't want to alarm her even more. She seemed troubled. Mother's face too was pained. She still had the remnants of rouge on her face and this gave her a mask-like appearance. Zosia had developed an infection in her leg and couldn't walk at all. The Germans told her to stay behind; they would send a truck to pick her and other infirm inmates up. She said she didn't trust them. "They will probably shoot me on the spot once everyone is gone." This was a strong possibility, and we decided not to leave her behind. The woman whose mother had died on the train volunteered to help, and so Zosia, supported on one side by Marysia and on the other by the still-crying young woman, limped along to the camp.

This must have been the longest twenty-minute walk ever. As we approached the barbed-wire fence, I was increasingly convinced that we had indeed made a mistake in choosing Germany over Poland. For the first time, we would be locked in, incarcerated by the Nazis. With all the turmoil and agony of the years in hiding, there had always been the illusion of freedom of choice, the possibility of running. Now, in ten minutes, we would be jailed, turned into anonymous numbers, at the mercy of vicious guards. The fear that we were being led to a concentration camp with gas chambers loomed even larger in my mind than the fear of losing freedom. I knew that the people who went to Auschwitz thought they were going to take showers, and instead of water, the Germans had turned on lethal gas. At what point did they know that this was the end? What signs should I be looking for? I was near panic.

9

The Shower

The camp itself was less ominous than I had feared. It was filled to capacity with thousands of refugees from Warsaw. Like Pruszków, it was divided into two parts. Here the division was predicated on hygienic issues: one section was for the arriving prisoners; the other was for those who had showered and been deloused, and were ready to be sent to work. We were assigned to cavernous barracks furnished with giant sleeping platforms on two levels. Each platform could accommodate at least twenty people. There were no mattresses or blankets. The place was spotless; the wooden planks scrubbed clean, the concrete floors without a speck of dirt.

Mother and Zosia stayed to watch our belongings while Lala, Marysia, and I went to assess the situation. I wanted to check out whether the other, so-called clean part of the camp really existed. I wanted to see whether the showers were real. Although it was already dark, we easily found the other part of the camp, which was divided from the rest by just a wire mesh fence. It was full of people who had passed through the cleaning process. We were in a legitimate labor camp; the Germans hadn't tricked us this time. Thankful, I embraced Lala.

I slept well that night, despite the hardness of the wooden berth. In the morning we got a full description of the camp's procedures. We were expected to wait a day or two for the move to the other side. From there we would be selected by German farmers or manufacturers and taken to our jobs, where we would be given sleeping quarters. It became obvious that we would have to make an all-out-effort if we were to get in touch with Rockschmidt: there were no phones in the camps and the guards seemed unapproachable. Then Mother, who spoke German better than the rest of us, approached one of the guards. She offered him her golden wedding ring if he would call Rockschmidt. This spurt of initiative was rare for her these days. We watched from a distance, holding our breaths. The guard promised to call and took the ring. The ring was our last valuable and we wondered about the wisdom of this move. What assurance did we have that he would do it? But it was a gamble we had to take.

To our surprise the German guard did call Rockschmidt. The same day! He brought back the news that Mother's former boss was dispatching Wuja, his uncle who had been the office manager in Warsaw, to pick us up and take us to his estate in Erzberg. Things were beginning to look up again.

The camp was a peculiar place. Interestingly enough, we were not afraid of the guards. The real threat was our fellow inmates. It seemed that the uprising and its overwhelming defeat at the hands of the Germans had totally demoralized the Polish youth. The five years of war, anarchy, and total absence of education culminated now in an outburst of random violence. Helpless against their real enemy, the Germans, and full of hatred and humiliation, young Polish men and women soon organized themselves into gangs that preyed on other inmates of the camp. Stealing and mugging were common during the day.

Once we found out what was going on, we started to look for a safe barrack, one with more middle-aged inmates and a higher percentage of men. As there was continual movement in and out of the camps, it was easy to shift from one place to another. On the second night Lala discovered what must have been the safest barrack on the premises. Out of eighty people there were at least forty-five men; and by design, there was one man near every woman. The gangs didn't bother us.

On the second day in camp, there was a sudden change in our situation. What had initially seemed an innocuous crossover to the clean part of the camp became, for me, the life-threatening experience of the whole war. As it turned out, the Germans were using the delousing procedure as a way to check whether the men were circumcised or not, to find Jews who might still be hiding among the refugees. We heard about it almost accidentally, when a Pole in our barrack said to Lala in a bragging tone, "I don't understand those Germans; I can recognize any of them just by looking at their faces." He proceeded to tell her that the Germans had caught four Jews the day before. The conversation was addressed to Lala, but I overheard it from where I was sitting. Although I doubted his skills, I slowly removed myself from his view. His story about the four Jews, however threw me into a panic. I started to shake all over, but made a superhuman effort to contain it. I wanted to leave the barrack, to walk or even run, but I was afraid of drawing the Pole's attention to myself. I had to lay down. From the ashen color of Lala's face, I realized that she must have felt as I did.

She was speechless for a short while and then answered the Pole in a voice that didn't sound like hers. "You are right. We have to catch them all. Have you looked around today?"

"No, but I'm going to do it now" was his answer. "Much as I hate Hitler," he continued, "we have to be grateful to him for what he has done to the Jews."

"G-d bless him for that," Lala answered.

He left. I felt faint. My sister came over and tried to reassure me by holding my hand, but no words were forthcoming. There was nothing to be said. She started to cry in silence, tears rolling down her cheeks. I knew what this meant. I was cornered this time. No plan could work under these circumstances. Lala kissed me and left to talk to Mother who was outside.

Still shaking I rested on the wooden planks and covered myself with Mother's coat. There were only two other people in the huge barrack, both sick. Everyone else was outside, sitting on the grass, warmed by the mellow fall sun. I wondered how much time I had left to live. One week, maybe two at best, if they took me to an extermination camp like Buchenwald or Ravensbrück. Auschwitz was already closed, as it was near the Russian frontier. Maybe I had only one day left. They might execute me just as they had killed my father. For the first time, I acknowledged that I had known from day one that he was dead, that he had been murdered by the Germans the day he'd been taken away. I wondered if he hadn't been luckier than I. By dying three years earlier he had avoided all the trials and agonies of Nazi occupation. I envied him for being already dead, while I still had to wait for my execution. Mother would not survive my death. She would deliver herself to the Germans. Maybe a year or two earlier she would have pulled through, but now she had lost her vitality. The events of the last five years had caught up with her emotionally. In our circumstances you didn't have to plan a suicide. Just tell the Germans, or maybe even your friendly neighbor, that you were a Jew, and it was over. She was at this point now.

I was perplexed by my reaction to what was happening. The possibility that I might be killed in a day or so, frightening as it had seemed at first, suddenly had an air of unreality about it. Did I really not care anymore? Why, then, the feeling of panic only moments before had it just been the suddenness of the latest developments? I had never believed in either G-d or life after death, but that day in the camp in Wilhelmshagen I wondered if it was at all possible that I might be reunited with Father. I had missed him very much in the years since his departure, but I had not allowed myself to dwell on such feelings. To be sentimental was to be vulnerable. Now, facing my own death, I was consoled somewhat by these thoughts of him.

Lala returned with Mother. They were crying, vainly trying to conceal their tears. For reasons not clear to me I felt an urge to console my mother, to cheer her up. It was almost as though it were my fault that they were going to kill me. I couldn't bear the idea that I was causing my mother additional pain. I told her not to worry; no doubt, I would outwit them once more. For the first time I talked about the Germans the way Captain Komarek had. I called them "the stupid Krauts." But of all the epithets I had used for the Germans, I knew that when it came to killing innocent people, this one was least applicable. Here their sophistication was beyond doubt. Anxiously, the three of us started to fabricate ploys for my survival during the delousing procedure. We were lying to each other, but this was the only way we could relate that last day of being together. Our barrack was to be vacated at ten o'clock the next morning.

None of us slept that night, but we remained silent, just tossing and turning. I wished something terrible would happen, an explosion, a fire. I even hoped one of the rape gangs might appear, anything that would dispel the frightening solitude of my last night.

Towards the morning, I felt nauseated. At around six I went out to throw up. Mother looked alarmed when I got up, but I reassured her that I was only going to the toilet.

We were the last ones to enter the showers, at 10:15. I kissed Mother and Lala, forcing a smile to my face. Without turning around, I went through the heavy steel door.

The place was immense; a cavernous steam bath with hundreds of showers spouting hot water on a huge crowd of naked bodies. The first step was to undress, to put all one's belongings into an individual wooden crate, take a towel, and proceed to the showers. The clothing went on a conveyor belt to a giant sterilizer, to be returned to us at the end of the cleaning procedure. I undressed slowly, trying to assess the situation, to figure out the system. It was important to find out the individual steps of the process. I was still looking for potential loopholes. It was difficult to see what was going on because of the masses of men milling around. The camp must previously have been used for processing the regular influx of forced laborers into Germany. Its facilities were now being overtaxed by the sudden arrival of thousands of captives from Warsaw, and it seemed to me that even the well-organized and methodical Germans were unable to cope with what was going on. I was somewhat encouraged by this, even without knowing yet what to do. Now I was nude, unprotected. I did have a towel, but no one was using them for cover. People where holding their shoulders. I crossed my arms on my chest and hung the towel casually in such a way that it covered me. Waiting for a free shower, I looked around for German guards, but to my surprise I couldn't find any. The main problem was to figure out what happened after the shower, what the next step was.

This was not the well-oiled Nazi death machine I had feared. It was a mind-boggling scene. I was encouraged by the pandemonium that ensued. There had to be a way to squeeze by unnoticed.

I took my shower and then moved cautiously to the area where the uniformed German officials were searching for lice in people's hair.

In such an atmosphere it was easy for me to skip the examination altogether. I slipped unnoticed into the next room, where I picked up my sterilized clothes. I was safe. I could not believe that this had really happened, how easy it had been!

I hurried to get dressed, knowing that Mother and Lala were waiting anxiously on the other side. They greeted me with disbelief and joy, their faces radiant with happiness. As it turned out, the guards were in the women's showers, but Mother and Lala told me that they hadn't cared. They had been totally preoccupied with their thoughts about me.

The "clean" side of the camp was quieter and better run than the other. The roaming gangs were gone, some of the members having been sent to a concentration camp as punishment for criminal activities. The sleeping arrangements were the same: giant two-story wooden platforms on both sides of the barrack. We had made friends on the other side – four lovely girls who we suspected might be Jews. They had been totally preoccupied with their thoughts about me.

Together with Zosia and Marysia we made a group of nine and occupied one upper platform. With four women on either side, I fell into a deep, well-deserved sleep. I had a very strange dream that night. I was in a beautiful marble palace, lying on a low bed made of cushions and Persian carpets.

Had it not been for the bad food, consisting mostly of tasteless turnip soup, our stay in Wilhelmshagen would have been a welcome respite at this point. Rockschmidt had notified the camp authorities that he would pick us up; it was only a matter of obtaining some official papers, which would take two or three days.

The camp routine had its predictable pace. After getting up in the morning, the inmates were expected to leave the barrack and gather on a large, grass-covered field. There around nine or ten o'clock, following the arrival of German factory managers and farmers, people were selected for their jobs, depending on what their future employers' needs were. The employers would walk around the premises and look over the inmates in this modern slave market. Although our jobs had already been designated, no one was allowed to stay in the barrack during the day, so we had to join the rest.

Zosia and Marysia were picked to work at the Schwarzkopf shampoo factory in Berlin. Our friends the four girls from Warsaw – Basia, Halinka, Ida, and Helena – also went to a factory in Berlin. They left, promising to visit us at Erzberg, Rockschmidt's estate. We would be free to travel in Germany on our days off.

Wuja arrived as promised. I had never met him before, and he looked somewhat surprised when he saw me for the first time. Mother had told him that I lived in the country with her sister, but my appearance now was the furthest imaginable from a country boys'. I was pale, very slim, malnourished, and tall for my age. My funny-looking clothes underscored my gawky appearance. Wuja was pleased to see Mother and very happy to be able to help. He felt guilty for having left Warsaw with his German nephew while we had to suffer through the two months of the uprising. "You fought for us all," were his first words. He had a chauffeured Mercedes limousine waiting for him, and both the Polish inmates and the German guards looked with surprise and envy at the way we were luxuriously departing from the labor camp. It must have been absolutely without precedent. We were going to Berlin by car and taking a two-hour train trip from there to Erzberg.

With tears in his eyes, Rockschmidt's Polish chauffeur said he felt honored to be able to drive the heroes of the Warsaw uprising. I just kept looking at the guards. What must have been going through their minds?

Seeing the Berlin of October 1944 was a heartwarming experience for me. The city was devastated: burned-out buildings; whole streets in ruins; sections cordoned off; the roads bombed, impassable, and caved in. Some areas were off-limits, as live bombs had not yet been disarmed because of the shortage of trained army engineers. The city was almost empty of men. Only here and there could one see elderly uniformed men guarding an occasional site or a street crossing. Wuja told us that they had been the last to be mobilized, and we were mockingly called Hitler's most precious army: silver on their heads, gold in their mouths, and lead in their legs. We drove through Berlin in Rockschmidt's beautiful Mercedes, taking in the sights.

On the train Wuja described the Erzberg estate; Gut Erzberg, as it was called in German. It was vast: seven hundred acres of arable land. The Rockschmidt's had eighty cows, twenty-odd horses, and numerous pigs, rabbits, and fowl. Mr. Rockschmidt was also raising pheasants as a hobby. The whole family was now living on the estate in an eighteen-room mansion. They had left their Berlin residence, fearing Allied bombs. They had two children: Beate, a twelve-year-old girl, and Wolfgang, a son who was just eighteen months old. There were also a grandmother, a sister, and several other relatives. The forced laborers, mostly Poles, but also Russians, French, and Dutch, lived in a former stable that had been converted into a dormitory. We were to be treated differently from the rest and given a room in the mansion.

Herr Rockschmidt was waiting for us at the railroad station. He seemed to give me a puzzled glance but maybe I was just self-conscious. He was obviously sentimental about Warsaw. His time there must have been the best of his life, and Mother was very much a part of that memory. In a sense, her competent management had made the whole operation possible.

We rode from the station in an elegant horse-drawn open carriage with Rockschmidt at the reins. He was extremely handsome – I had seen only his photograph before – six foot two, blond, and athletic. He wore a riding outfit with a hat and boots. Having seen the decrepit, aging men of Berlin just a few hours before, I kept wondering how he had been able to stay out of the army when everyone else from sixteen to sixty-five had been mobilized. Wuja later explained that our boss had gotten an exemption from the service because of his company's importance to the war effort; but this was only a part of the story. His connections and bribes to important Nazi party official had helped to ensure that the waiver was maintained. I was surprised to hear all this. I guess I had a tendency to overestimate the Nazis.

Erzberg was grander than I had imagined from its descriptions. The mansion was of palatial proportions. Its circular driveway, immaculate lawn, and the pristine white of the building made an overwhelming impression, probably more so because of the damage and destruction I had witnessed both in Warsaw and in Berlin. We arrived late in the day and were given a cheerfully appointed room with two beds in the guest wing. Mother shared a bed with Lala. I had my own. My first mattress in G-d knew how many weeks. It felt luxurious.

Mrs. Rockschmidt was tall and obese. She looked older than her husband: a typical German hausfrau. She was very friendly and kind. Upon seeing me she suggested that I might have incipient TB. She told the cook to give me extra-large portions of nourishing food, including three glasses of whole milk a day – an unheard of luxury in 1944 Germany. The milk ration in the cities was one glass a week, for children only. Her suggestion immediately caused friction with her mother-in-law, a nasty, dried-out old lady who seemed to be the real power wielder of the Rockschmidt household.

Later that day, we were assigned our work. Mother's job was that of an assistant cook. There were eighteen to twenty people to be fed daily, and the cook Jadwiga, also a Pole, needed help. Lala became the Kinderfräulein to baby Wolfgang, and I was sent to be a cowherd, tending a herd of twenty-five heifers that grazed behind the stable. My exposure to cows before that day had been limited to seeing them through the window of a moving train when I was eight or nine years old and we were going to the resort town of Jaremcze. I used to lean against the train's window with Lala and count the cows; year after year my father would repeat the joke about the mathematician who was told to count sheep from a moving train. Having done it in less than a second he was asked about his method. "It's simple," was his answer. "I count their legs and divide by four." Now, as I stood in front of the men in charge of the stable, this joke was all I could think of. I was nervous.

I was already used to people's first reaction when they saw me: the combination of pity and mild revulsion at my gawky, pale, and pimply look but Stefan, the Polish stable foreman, could not contain his laughter and called in his assistant, "Come, see who is going to be in charge of the heifers." Now both were roaring with laughter, slapping their thighs. "Are you going to read them fairy tales, Panie Intelligent?" Stefan continued in a rather primitive Polish, after he had controlled his laughter.

"Panie Intelligent," roughly, "egghead," became my nickname for the rest of my stay in Erzberg. I didn't know what to answer, whether to be humble or to brag. I decided to show him that I wasn't as inexperienced as he presumed and retorted, "When do you want me to bring them back for milking?"

I thought both would die laughing. "The skeleton thinks that heifers have to be milked!" Stefan sputtered between cascades of laughter. "That's too much."

I was on the verge of tears but managed to control myself. I was shown my charges and the area they would graze. I was told to report at 5:00 the next morning.

The first day was hard for all three of us. Lala was confused, also on the verge of tears, having been given directives by three different women – the mother-in-law, the sister-in-law, and Wolfgang's mother – on how to care for the little boy, who was treated like the crown prince. Mother, on the other hand, was exhausted. She had spent the day peeling vats of potatoes, the main staple of those days, and scrubbing an endless array of pots and pans while being constantly criticized by the cook, Jadwiga, and the senior Mrs. Rockschmidt. But despite our travails, we were in excellent spirits, thankful that these were our only concerns.

The next morning I went with Wojtek, Stefan's assistant, to take the heifers out. I realized that I had worried too much the day before. The calves were busy grazing. When they strayed into a place that was off-limits, Wojtek would whack them with a long reed to make them return to the assigned area. I spent most of the day basking in the still-warm October sun, relishing the beauty of the countryside.

The problems started the next day, after Wojtek was gone. Started is probably too mild a word; exploded would be more appropriate. Early in the day, I realized that the pasture was strategically located between the sugar beets and the apple orchard. This meant that the heifers would either wander off into the beets or stray toward the fruit trees. Both areas were forbidden. Their behavior was almost predictable. Hardly had I prevented them from munching on the delicious ripe apples than they were chewing on the beets, plucking them out by their green leaves. My reed caused them little or no pain, and to be honest, I was afraid to get close enough to give them a good whacking. I started to throw stones at them with equally limited results. Only years later, after reading Erikson, did I realize that heifers are in reality adolescent cows, and should be treated with some understanding rather than brute force. That was not alarming evidence of their savagery, as I had supposed. Needless to say, I was near exhaustion at the end of the day, totally incapable of getting my herd back to the barn.

Things got better after a week, but Mrs. Rockschmidt senior complained to her son that all the apples had been eaten in the northern part of the orchard, and I was transferred to another job. As it turned out later, the blame was unfairly placed; the apples had been stolen by the

Polish laborers. Not having intended to become a professional cowherd, I didn't take the unjust accusation of incompetence to heart.

I gained weight rapidly and, by the end of the month, was assigned to the silo where grain was stored. I had to carry bags weighing fifty pounds up two stories. To my surprise, I started to enjoy the work after a few days, and I began to feel physically fit for the first time in my life.

The fact that we lived in the owner's mansion, and that both Mother and Lala worked there, gave me a privileged position among the estate's foreign laborers. Rockschmidt's patronage eliminated the suspicion that we might be Jewish. The difference between us and the rest of the workers was ascribed to our belonging to a different social class, and not to race or religion. There were rumors, we were told by Wuja, that my mother was an aristocrat who, having had an out-of-wedlock child (Lala still bore a different last name) was forced to work as a domestic. We felt safe.

My jobs kept changing with the demands of the season. I was quickly becoming a full-fledged farmhand. After the silo, I was assigned to carting hay from the fields in a giant wagon pulled by two oxen. As each job necessarily had a different challenge and new problems, I stopped worrying about not being able to cope. The trouble with oxen, for example, was their stubbornness. Two of us drove the hay wagon: Lolek, who was also fourteen, and I. Lolek was supposed to be the experienced one. He had come to Erzberg with his parents three years earlier and had worked there ever since. As it turned out, however, experience didn't count with the oxen. It was ingenuity, a talent for improvisation that mattered. Day after day we were at a loss as to what to do when the oxen, pulling the heavy wagon, suddenly stopped in their tracks. No amount of lashing with a horse whip would make them budge. Pleading and carrots were to no avail. Only a wicked idea of mine had the desired effect. I lit a stick and placed it, burning, under the poor beast's tail. To everybody's surprise we rode swiftly to the barn ahead of the others. We did not reveal our trade secret to anyone.

If I had any vestige of childhood innocence left by the time I arrived in Erzberg – which I doubt – it disappeared rapidly on the estate. After five years of war, life in slave-like conditions had totally destroyed any semblance of human decency and morals among the captive laborers. Deprived of humane living conditions: men, women and children of all ages, some of whom had been born in captivity, they were treated relatively well. There was no physical abuse, as this was not a labor or concentration camp. Still, they had no rights: no days off, no pay except food. They spent their free time drinking an alcoholic brew they managed to produce behind Rockschmidt's back. I seldom visited the workers' stable; we didn't belong there.

In mid-November Herr Rockschmidt announced that the following week we would not be working in the fields for two days; we would participate in a hunt for wild rabbits. He had invited several of his close friends, high Nazi officials and Gestapo officers, to spend two days in the country. The captive workers, together with dogs, were to assist the hunt by rounding up rabbits. Even Mother, who didn't talk much in those days, expressed her surprise at the boss's idea. The Russians were deep inside Poland, almost on the German border. The Allies in the west were moving swiftly. Berlin was in shambles, the German people on the verge of starvation, eating weeds as farm supplies dwindled. And here we were to stop working and help the Nazi elite in a rabbit hunt.

The eight of them shot three rabbits. We chased the rest in the opposite direction when no one was watching. The hunters didn't care. They were already drunk at ten in the morning after a breakfast that included caviar brought by one of the guests, Russian vodka, and exquisite French champagne supplied by the host from his private cellar. With their beer bellies bulging from under their party uniforms, they could hardly mount the horses. I had spent the whole morning, from five o'clock onward, grooming the horses to perfection; one of the fat, aging Germans whom I helped climb into his saddle gave me one mark as a tip. Their women, or rather, their girls, for they were all very young stayed behind, doting on little Wolfgang, who, at the orders of the boss, was dressed in a blue velvet suit with a lace collar.

Mrs. Rockschmidt did not approve of the hunt. She described it as a decadent and macabre idea and spent the day in bed feigning a migraine headache. Mother told us about the fight between our boss and his wife; she had overheard it the day before the hunt. Mrs. Rockschmidt, who was eight years older than her husband was also better educated and more sophisticated. There was a barrage of mutual insults during the argument.

I helped skin the rabbits, and Mother roasted them together with a suckling pig we had slaughtered the night before. This was another of our boss's illicit deeds. All animals had to be registered with the authorities in charge of food supplies. A newborn calf or pig was to be reported the same day and given an earring with a number. Such animals could not be sold or slaughtered without permission. Since the police could not know how many animals were born on a specific day, especially pigs, which have multiple offspring in a litter, we would report the birth a day later and slaughter one or two suckling pigs at night. Tadek was the resident butcher, and later in the year I became his assistant.

Mother got sick immediately after the hunt. She was overworked and exhausted. It was more than a week before she was back on her feet, and she was still very weak and needed a great deal of rest. Lala and I took her for walks for some exercise, some fresh air. We also hoped that the pleasant country sights would lift her spirits. She hardly responded to our efforts. As soon as we would go to the village, she would insist on stopping in front of every one of the several churchyards on our way. Leaning against the fence she would say each time, "You will bury me here. This is my last stop." She looked like a shadow of her former self. Having lost almost half of her prewar weight, she was just over eighty pounds. Lala thought Mother never recovered from the anxiety that we might have been killed when we were separated from her during the Warsaw uprising. My experiences in the camp at Wilhelmshagen were an additional blow with which she could not cope. Fortunately Mrs. Rockschmidt did not insist upon her immediate return to work, and this allowed Mother to slowly regain her equilibrium.

10

Triumph

It is Christmas, 1944. "Stille Nacht, Heilige Nacht." We are sitting in our boss's lavishly furnished living room, singing Christmas carols before an eight-foot tree. The walls are covered with paintings of family ancestors. Hitler's picture, which hung there during the hunt, is gone. We are the only laborers invited to the party. Herr Rockschmidt is wearing a cutaway. His frilled mauve shirt is adorned with diamond cuff links. His wife is dressed in a long, black, rather old fashioned velvet dress with a string of pearls around her neck. The twelve-year-old Beate looks like a princess in her blue taffeta dress. She also wears braces. She is as ugly as her mother. Beate's baby brother, Wolfgang, in a velvet suit with an embroidered lace collar, is sitting on his father's lap. The rest of the family – the boss's mother, his sister, and his brother-in-law – look equally festive. The sister's husband is wearing an army uniform. The right sleeve of his jacket is empty, the only reminder that this is Germany in the sixth year of war. The table is groaning under the weight of the food. Two roasted suckling pigs with baked apples in their snouts. Traditional delicacies, vegetables and fruits galore. Champagne unlimited. I'm overwhelmed by all this. I can't take it. Six years! I should have been free by now. Ironically, this is the first time in all those years that I have been invited to a family Christmas dinner. It bothers me that the Germans around me are having such a joyous time, benevolently tolerating our presence. Isn't there ever going to be justice? Beate is the one who bothers me most. Almost a contemporary of mine, she hasn't greeted me once in the three months at Erzberg, not even answered my "Guten morgen." I do not exist for her. I am a creature from the lower race, a primitive Pole.

Herr Rockschmidt offers a toast. He talks about the importance of family life and the need for peace. I have a strong feeling of disdain for him. Thank G-d for the champagne. It makes an event like this somewhat more palatable.

A week later Mother removed the Christmas decorations. Mrs. Rockschmidt urged her to remember where she was putting each item, to make it easier to find them next year. When Mother told us about it in the evening, we didn't know whether to laugh or cry. Who was being foolish, we or they? Was it possible that the war would last another year? Did they know something that we didn't? It was true the Russians hadn't moved much on the Eastern front since the uprising. But this had been their pattern; an offensive and then several months to catch up with the supplies. Anyway, they preferred fighting in the winter, so something should be happening soon.

Mrs. Rockschmidt's remark left us without peace of mind. But three weeks later – January 22, 1945 – the Soviets, under the brilliant Marshal Zhukov, smashed the German defenses and conquered Warsaw. Four months later this new offensive would get them Berlin. Now our roles were reversed. The boss and his family listened anxiously to the news from the BBC. Their bad news was our good news. I relished the mounting anxiety in their eyes each time the radio announced Allied advances on the front. This time our victory was near.

It was admirable how so many Poles I had met during this war – Mietek, Mrs. Krawczyk's nephew executed on the streets of Warsaw; Captain Komarek, the leader of the march in the sewers; Captain Jarecki, who had delivered the beautiful eulogy for Janek; had this unique and enviable ability to face death as a matter-of-fact reality, a part of life. I was determined to follow their example in my next brush with danger.

The events of the ensuing weeks followed a predictable pattern. Every day, it seemed, another important German city fell into either Soviet or Allied hands. We were now equidistant from the two fronts, and we had daily proof of how close the end of the war was. During the morning Russian reconnaissance planes, usually in pairs, flew low over Rockschmidt's estate, taking aerial pictures and occasionally strafing passing vehicles with machine guns. We gave the planes the affectionate nicknames: Sasha and Vanya, after the two Russian workers on the estate. When they passed overhead, we would stop working and, oblivious to the danger, applaud our "friends", sending them kisses through the air. Our German supervisors frowned as they searched the skies in vain for the Luftwaffe Messerschmitt to chase the "Ruskies" away.

At night we watched the light-and-sound show from Berlin, in the west. The skies were as bright as in daytime, illuminated by vast numbers of flares suspended from parachutes dropped by Allied planes. Once the target became visible, thousands of bombs were dropped nightly on the German capital. The thud of explosions, music to my ears carried for miles, rattling the windows of the estate's mansion.

With the end of the war imminent, we could measure the Allies' progress on the front by the behavior of our bosses. To call their attitude toward us friendly would be an understatement. Loving might be more appropriate. Mrs. Rockschmidt insisted now on helping Mother in the kitchen. "You look tired, Meine Stasia" was her favorite expression. I was told to quit and go play with Beate. I was too young to work, they claimed. Lala was asked to continue taking care of little Wolfgang. "He loves you more than he does his mother," was the comment. Now we ate our meals in the dining room with the boss's mother serving.

I vented all my anger on little Beate. When we played ball, I aimed at her face; in hide-and-seek I would trip her when she was about to find me. Her parents turned a deaf ear to her complaints about me, and I would call her a liar to their faces. By now the idea of playing was so foreign to me that I couldn't enjoy it at all. Strangely, I felt more at ease working. Making Beate's life miserable was my only fun.

We celebrated my fifteenth birthday on March 31, four weeks to the day before we were liberated. Mrs. Rockschmidt baked a cake, and poor Beate decorated it with candles. They handed me a present, a beautiful hand-knitted sweater, and the whole family sang the German version of "Happy Birthday." I glanced at Mother and Lala. We knew that this was the moment of our greatest personal victory. Eight Germans cheering a Jew who had outwitted them all! A far cry from my fourteenth "Petronius's feast" birthday! I felt powerful and victorious. Herr Rockschmidt was sober in his toast. "This war, if anything, should teach us that the roles of victims and victors are interchangeable." I understood what he meant. I was ready for the change. Was he?

The first Russian soldiers arrived on April 28, 1945. It would sound strange to say that they came unexpectedly. Hadn't we been waiting for them for the last four years? But that was how it happened: their arrival took us by surprise. We hadn't seen any German soldiers for several days, and we thought the front was at least ten or twenty miles away. But the Red Army was already west of us, between Erzberg and Berlin. By the time the soldiers arrived we had already been under Russian rule for three or four days. At first I felt let down. I had no preconceived notion of what form my liberation would take. Nevertheless, discovering that we had been free for several days without knowing it was anticlimactic.

The four Russian officers looked rugged, tough and self-assured. They drove in an American-made Jeep. Their uniforms were messy, and their faces were fatigued. They seemed more seasoned then I remembered the Russians being in 1941. The war had matured us all. When they entered the mansion, Rockschmidt was shaking, leaning against the wall. He seemed to need it for support. His eyes were fearful. He was trying to force a smile, but his lips were quivering.

The Soviets were unexpectedly friendly and easygoing. Mother and Lala acted as interpreters. The Russians wanted to drink a toast to victory, to Stalin. They brought their own vodka, a powerful potion of the highest possible proof. Mother suggested mixing it with water, but they refused. I was observing our boss – or shall I call him our former boss? Before my eyes flashed another scene, almost identical except for the characters.

It's January 1940. We are subletting my parents' bedroom by military order and without pay to a Soviet couple. He is a lieutenant – very young, maybe twenty – stationed with his wife in Lwów. Her name is Natasha. She's charming, all smiles, and eyes full of kindness. Their spirits are high. They insist we celebrate the liberation of Lwów from capitalist oppression and drink to Stalin. My poor father, as pale as Rockschmidt is now, is being offered that same powerful vodka. He has never had vodka before. Father looks pleadingly to Mother, at a loss. We all laugh as Father slips out of the room. We find him later in the bathroom, vomiting.

No one came to Rockschmidt's rescue. Mother, Lala and I watched impassively as he toasted Stalin, his face red as a beet in reaction to the potent alcohol. His wife and all the German women in the household were hiding somewhere in the mansion. The officers asked Lala where she had learned Russian. Upon hearing that we were slave laborers from eastern Poland, they became sullen. One of them said deploringly, "So that's how it is. We were fighting the Nazis and you were helping them." This statement came unexpectedly. It threw us into shock. Was that what they thought of us? Did this mean that our liberators considered us traitors? Lala repeated what she had told the officers before, hoping there had been some misunderstanding, but they ignored her completely. They got up, shook hands with Rockschmidt, and left without looking in our direction.

That day several other Red Army jeeps appeared on the estate. The soldiers were less friendly, interested only in the horses and stables. They took the animals one by one, leaving only the very young.

Rockschmidt's Mercedes was taken the following day as were two VWs and several trucks that were part of his moving company. He didn't react. We all knew that this was just the beginning, that each arrival of a group of Russian soldiers would mean another loss, another requisition.

The Rockschmidts decided not to leave, but to make a hideaway for the women. It was built in the silo under a gigantic stack of sacks full of grain. On the third day we heard that the German telephone operators, all nine of them, had committed suicide by hanging. Little though we pitied the Germans, we found this last news unsettling. There was an element of frenzy in the behavior of the Russian soldiers, justified perhaps by the horrible four years of fighting, but objectively excessive and potentially dangerous for all of us. We were eager to leave as soon as possible for Poland. We decided to leave Erzberg the next day in the direction of Poland. There was no way of getting over to the Americans in the west. Berlin hadn't fallen and the war wouldn't be over for another few days. But we were afraid to wait among the Germans. At all costs, we had to avoid being identified by the Soviets as Nazi collaborators.

The following morning we told Rockschmidt that we were leaving. We also revealed to all, for the first time, that we were Jews. Their reaction was puzzling. After the initial expression of surprise Rockschmidt recalled that back in Warsaw one of his Gestapo friends had commented that Mother looked too refined and too cultured to be a maid. He had suggested that Rockschmidt contact Gestapo headquarters and have them investigate the matter. He didn't. Now he wanted credit for that, implying that he had saved our lives. I was not convinced by this story. I was sure that he wouldn't have kept Mother if he had really suspected she was Jewish. Nevertheless, we were living in times when one had to be grateful to another human being for not exercising his option to kill. It was true: he could have had Mother exterminated. It was confusing. Should one really be grateful to a driver for not running one over when he could have done it with impunity? Benevolence by omission?

Mrs. Rockschmidt started to cry. She asked Lala to take Wolfgang back with her to Poland. He would be safer with us. Mother refused. She couldn't do that to Lala, she said; people would assume that Wolfgang was her out-of-wedlock child. Mother suggested, instead, that it might be a good idea for Mrs. Rockschmidt to claim to be of Jewish descent. We might give her some help in establishing a Jewish background. "Julek will write you a Hebrew letter." Mrs. Rockschmidt was visibly shocked and indignant at this suggestion. "Stasia! How dare you suggest and idea like that!" She recovered seconds later and said apologetically, "I mean, it would be too difficult to implement that very helpful suggestion."

The exchange didn't surprise me. They didn't yet comprehend the seriousness of their predicament. They didn't understand what it meant to lose a war to the Russians. I knew that it wouldn't be long before they found out.

So it was time again for packing. G-d knows how many times we had done it since that fateful autumn of 1939. Each time there had been less to pack, our belongings dwindling and their importance becoming secondary to survival. I was in a hurry to get out of there, to return to circumstances that would at least have a semblance of normality, to start searching for my father. Maybe, after all, he had somehow survived that mass execution on Petliura day. Maybe they had taken him to the Austrian coal mines after all.

We took a britzka with the only horse left in the stable, a two-year-old mare that hadn't been trained yet to pull a carriage and had therefore been left behind by the Russians. Mother would sit on the britzka while Tadek would hold the reins, walking on the side so as not to overburden the inexperienced animal. Lala and I were to ride bicycles behind the wagon.

We had only one suitcase, graciously donated by our former boss. It was more than enough for what we had brought from Warsaw. They allowed me to take Beate's Peugeot bicycle, which her daddy had bought her a year before in Paris. For the first time in my life I was riding a bicycle; it suddenly felt as though my childhood were beginning afresh.

The farewell was very emotional. All the Rockschmidt's were crying. Mother and Lala had tears in their eyes. I was unmoved. I knew that they were not crying because we were leaving. Our departure signified the end of a glorious period in their lives, lives of luxury – at our expense. I thought Mrs. Rockschmidt had laughed too early in Warsaw, in June 1944, when she rejoiced that her husband would be "little Hansi" again after having been "der Grosse Herr" for all those years. She hadn't known then that it would also entail her becoming "little Berta" whose seven hundred acres would be the plundering ground for the victorious Red Army.

We were on our way home, although we couldn't imagine what home meant at this point in our lives. We were all happy except the horse, who was having a hard time adjusting to her first job. The driver had a supply of sugar cubes in his pocket, and he would alternate between the whip and the sweets.

Mother was napping on the slow-moving britzka. I was riding behind the cart on my bike next to Lala, absorbed in my thoughts, full of conflicting emotions. I was thinking of all the people who probably hadn't survived the war: Father; my little cousin Juleczek; Arthur and Sonia, his parents; Ludwig; my aunts and uncles; my many cousins. I hoped that some of them had been as lucky as we. I also thought of how I would be going back to school. I wouldn't have to lie and pretend anymore. Soon we might be able to join our family in Palestine... 5 Jabotinsky Street, Tel Aviv.

The Gruenfeld Family

The roads were crowded. The Russian army – tanks, artillery, and infantry – were still moving west toward Berlin in huge numbers, while thousands of former slave laborers were going east toward Poland and Russia. According to Soviet officers, there were trains waiting in Frankfurt an Der Oder, about a hundred miles away, for the refugees returning to Poland. It should not take us more than two days to get there.

The Soviets continued to be hostile to returning refugees. Two hours after we left Erzberg, our bikes were taken away without explanation and without comment. Lala, Tadek the driver, and I walked behind the britzka. The horse could hardly pull the cart with Mother in it. Toward noon, the horse was requisitioned by a passing Soviet cavalry unit. There was no use resisting. We were forced to stop while Tadek and Lala went in search of a pushcart. They returned with one a short while later. It must have been left behind by some of the German refugees who were fleeing west en masse, hoping to enter American-occupied territory once the war was over. The cart still had their possessions on it.

We transferred our belongings to the pushcart and started slowly on our way, Tadek and I pulling the cart, Mother and Lala pushing it from behind. It was hard work, and we were saddened by the treatment we were receiving from the Russians. It wasn't the victorious return home we thought we deserved after all those tragic years.

An hour later a soldier took my heavy shoes. He was apologetic, showing me his, which were in shreds. He needed shoes to keep fighting the Germans, he said shaking my hand in appreciation. I didn't mind anymore. Such a war doesn't end in one day. I wrapped my feet in a cut-up shirt and we continued on our march east.

I was remembering our trip toward the Romanian border in September 1939. I saw Father in his elegant fur-trimmed coat and his brown Borsalino hat, Mother in her luxurious Chanel-like suit, Lala and myself in our Shabbos best. It all seemed centuries ago, a luxurious cruise from which none of us would ever return.

Part Two
Lala's Story

Mama

She was, and she still is here alive
And with us for all generations.

Like the kind fairy from tales of yore,
Whoever knew her was able to thoughtfully say,
How good it was to be in her presence.

She was not one to say much or use many words;
Rather she listened, and understood and helped,
With advice, actions, and by
Attaching herself and binding herself to all . . .
To everyone, young and old alike.

And at the end when there were no more words . . .
She lay in her bed, quietly composed and relaxed,
Without suffering
She gazed at us with her beautiful blue eyes
And her caress taught us those lessons
Which will guide us and escort us for many years to come.

Lala's Diary

Written during the Polish Uprising in Warsaw, 1944

By
Ilana (Lala) Weinreb Levron

A page from Lala's diary. The German slogan reads: Besser zehn worte zu wenig als ein wort zu viel – Better ten words less than one word too much.

Lala's diary is preserved in the archives of the Massuah Institute for the Study of the Holocaust at Kibbutz Tel Yitzhak, where it was translated.

WHO AM I ?

Warsaw 1-8-44

The Germans have left the city. My boss, Herbert Schmoll, (a dentist from Bremen, Gemany who employed me as his assistant in his dental practice on 5 Sejmowa Street in Warsaw, was a Gestapo agent. During aktions in the Warsaw Ghetto he would close his practice and volunteer his efforts to willingly exterminate Jews. This explanation does not appear in the original diary because it was written while in hiding.) and many other employers have also left as well. It means nothing to me that they got out just in the nick of time. With German precision they succeeded in escaping the "hand of justice and vengeance," which would have surely struck them after such a vicious and cruel five years of oppression and tyranny as conquerors [of this city].

The very fact that Warsaw has been liberated and is "Deutschen-Frei," (free of the Germans) fills my heart with joy. It is still hard for me to believe that I will never hear again, "Halina, where did you spend your free time this past Sunday? You are always full of secrets. It seems suspicious to me. Aren't you in fact part of the underground?"

Is my role which I have faithfully played all these years truly over? Has the end really come to the fear and terror of what tomorrow will bring? Is it true?

Today I went in the morning to visit Irka and Kazik (the Laskys [Zilberbergs] were a Jewish couple who were my friends from the city of Częstochowa. They hid in Warsaw under Aryan papers and survived the Holocaust. In 1956, he lost his position as a professor in a Polish university and he moved to Graz, Austria.) in order to bring them some food. The German Shmidts (A German family from Berlin who employed my mother as a housekeeper. Their actions and conduct were humane. They are the Rockschmidts in Part One) who employed my mother as a housekeeper and assistant left her upon their escape with a storage room filled with various food stuffs. I wanted to bring my friends who lived on Wolska Street, some food, so that they should be prepared in case of a shortage. Such a shortage could surprise us at any moment since the Soviet army is only a 25km distance away from Warsaw at the moment. They are just over the Vistula river and quickly traveling in this direction at a rate of some thirty kilometers a day.

As usual I was received at Irka's with a lively heartfelt smile. We were overjoyed to be reunited once more. Even though Irka and Kazik live in a dark basement apartment, it was here that together we passed our own great moments, arguments flared and lively discussions ensued between us on universal subjects; the eternal problems of mankind and we lived there basking in the radiance of an invisible sun that was not there, as Irka described it in one of her poems.

Because of the tense situation, I promised my mother that I would be back that very day. But fate had it otherwise . . .

At five in the afternoon we heard from the direction of Chmielna Street the first sounds of gun fire.

Immediately I understood that the uprising and rebellion had begun. True none of us were aware that precisely on that very day the uprising would begin, however the city was prepared and waiting for this moment.

I was very upset that I was cut off from my home and that I would only be able to return once everything ended peacefully. In addition to all this I did not find Kazik at home, and Irka was worried that they too would be separated and cut off from each other. Later that evening as we sat by the little window in their basement apartment filled with fear and terror, our ears attuned to the sounds and echoes of approaching gun shots and worse – the echoes of the tank mortars from the Tigers, Kazik burst in like a whirlwind into the room with a young girl, who was a stranger at his heels. A long moment passed until they had calmed down enough to tell us the details of their adventures. And so it was: When the first shots that rang out surprised them and caught them off guard they ran into the hallway of one of the buildings. Quickly the streets emptied of passersby. When the gunfire ceased, they left their hiding place and ventured to look outside walking slowly step by step in the direction of home. On their way they passed two victims. The sight of the first casualties shocked them however the distance to reach home was small. They decided despite the imminent danger that they would run from house to house. A few courageous souls got up the courage to join them and they followed in their footsteps, some with their hands raised high in a gesture of surrender, however the majority were too terrified from the sight of the first victims [to follow us].

As darkness descended onto our small room we continued sitting on the bed, by the window, near one another concentrating on the echoing sounds of gun shots. And separately each one of us dreamed each his own personal dream ... a vision of freedom, whose sparks had been ignited towards reality.

2-8-44

I went out onto the street with Irka. Our eyes met with an unbelievable sight: Small children distributing the newspaper of the rebellion. For the first time in five years we could proudly read a Polish newspaper that was printed and distributed officially and openly. Down Wolska Street our own Polish soldiers marched in two rows. They were off course still wearing civilian clothes however they each wear a red and white armband emblazoned with the letters W.P. [that stand for Wojska Polskiego] (Polish Army). Irka playfully pinches my arm to divert my attention to two army medics with armbands emblazoned with the red cross on them, first aid kits strung over their shoulders and Polish eagle symbols on their shirts. "Those are courageous girls!" says the elderly guard who stands at the gate as we look on in agreement. Everyone is called on to volunteer to dig trenches to help guard us. Kazik is one of the first volunteers. We are sure he will no longer be home. Off course that's not really his place to be.

3-8-44

Being cut off from home is beginning to depress me. All day long all I could think about was how to get in touch with my mother, how could I try and contact her? I imagine how sad and upset she must be and how she must worry in her solitude all alone.

Jasia, one of Kazik's acquaintances who is living with us now also dreams of getting in touch with her division and her family. I already have a few ideas which I will try out tomorrow. The newspapers announced today that several important public buildings have also been captured. The atmosphere is simply wonderful and our morale is high.

4-8-44

You, my beloved have always determined that I have such great Mazal. Perhaps you are right. Mazal is a lofty word, more sophisticated than the truth, but somehow I succeed (when I truly wish and try to.)

Today I went out into the street with Kazik to try and contact my mother somehow. Irka said that I would end up getting arrested with my wild ideas and Kazik who accompanied me since he was worried for me to go out alone, simply shook his head in doubt. Imagine their admiration when I returned after having successfully carried out my mission. My plan was thus: Until the rebellion broke out the only telephone lines in operation were owned by the Germans. Since the Polish army conquered their police command building which stood on Żelazna Street I imagined, correctly, that the phones lines had not yet been cut and thereby I could communicate with my mother (by simply calling her on the phone) since she was living on a German [controlled] street. However how could I get a permit from the Polish army for a private matter such as this without arousing suspicions that I was a spy? Such suspicions were the same that Irka harbored and they were not unfounded, many of the citizens of Warsaw were Folksdeutsche (Poles with German ancestry) who engaged in spying.

The presence among us of snipers, who shot from the rooftops and windows of private homes, at the populace was also proof of spies. The work of the snipers was one of the most difficult blows to the rebellion. No one could catch them, because they were scattered all over the city and they fought against us in many non humanitarian ways such as using expanding bullets also known as dumdums.

You can imagine for yourself how I felt like such a brave girl when despite all the warnings I entered the former police station. At the gate the patrolman stopped me and asked for identification papers and to state the purpose of my visit and what requests I had. When they heard my request they were speechless. "You want to make a phone call today? OK go ahead and try, who knows if you will even have a line or connection? However first we need to contact Lieutenant Klein." After a long wait I stood before the Lieutenant. If not for the various insignias sewn onto his black shirt, testifying to his rank I would never have imagined I was standing before an officer. All his actions, mannerisms and manner of speech would have otherwise led me to believe I was speaking with one of the lowlife hooligans from the Wolska district who we called "Andrews". Afterwards I discovered that my initial judgment was in fact correct. Lt. Klein was in fact raised in the Wolska district known for its notorious reputation and all his ranks were in fact awarded for the bravery which he displayed in the mission conquering the former police station. On his conscience to date were three dead Germans. And he regarded me and my request in a very positive light. He pointed to the telephone and just to be on the safe side he sent another soldier with me to eavesdrop on my conversation. With growing excitement I dialed the number on the phone. Accompanied by heavy heart beats I waited for the connection. And then suddenly I heard my mother's voice ask: "Is it you?!"

There is no way my emotions can be put into words. From a few short sentences I understood what was happening with her, they were constantly under a hail of bullets, the shots rained down upon them from the Y.M.C.A. street. It was difficult for her to believe we were walking about freely in the streets. They spent the entire time in their shelters. Mother objected to the fact that we were separated. She felt alone and left behind. Tadzik and Maria are with her (they too were caught and surprised by the outbreak of the rebellion) however she claimed that only I could help her at least to lift her morale. I had to, to my chagrin and sorrow, end the conversation even though it is so difficult for me to bid farewell to Mother. Will I ever hear her voice ever again? I leave the building, walk out the gate and look for Kazik. He is gone, The streets are empty. I see passing above me in the skies, enemy Stuka planes. I run to the gate so as to avoid becoming a target for their fire. In the hallway of the building I meet Kazik. He blesses my successes.

Jasia succeeded in establishing contact with her division. She is a member of the Armia Ludowa – the people's army which went out to battle on the second day of the rebellion. Based on the newspapers' reports, it was possible to understand that there was some sort of united front of fighters against our common enemy. However if you read between the lines and listen to the talk on the street, you could sense the sensitive disagreements between the Armia Krajowa and the Armia Ludowa (between the National Army and the People's Army).

Yasha is a liaison officer. Today she began her job. She runs through the city passing orders and commands. Kazik asks her to include him as well. He claims that men are needed to bear arms. There is a surplus of women.

Kazik has left and we are alone. We deluded ourselves into believing he would be back this evening, but he did not return. All day long we waited – for nothing. The newspapers reported new victories. The Old City and the city center were now under the control of our army, in the Wolska district – battles raged on. We knew this all too well, since the German tank that was located not far from us on Chlodna Street keeps firing non-stop. Today was a difficult day for me, not just because at home the atmosphere is one of panic and fright, but also because several houses on Karolkowa Street and Building number 5 on Wolska Street are up in flames. This means that Germans are coming closer towards us. I am still under the spell of the conversation with my mother and I cannot stop thinking about it. It was a miracle that I even got connected, because the Germans who conquered the telephone and communications center severed and disconnected all the lines, and it was a great coincidence that I found one phone that actually worked! I do not know, and I do not want to even imagine how difficult is must be for heart this moment. My mother's home is surrounded by burning buildings, from the sides of Prachkati, Wiejska Streets. The Germans are entering those buildings and taking out people and taking them, we know not where to. I know that my mother is always calm and collected in all situations, if she is so depressed it must be that the situation is hopeless. I asked if there was any hope of escape but the answer I received was negative. Every plan was thought of and argued over by the inhabitants of building number 5 on Konopnicka Street, however none of them was possible to carry out since they were under house arrest. The worst thing is the fact that on the Minsterman factory's lot which is very close, there are three giant gasoline tanks. If they should be accidentally hit there could be a potential disaster! The danger continues to mount as the grenades continue to explode in all directions.

7-8-44

All day and all night long the tank's cannons roared. Our house on Chlodna Street was in a panic. All the houses around us are already on fire. Since we live on the ground floor all the other inhabitants of the building are gathering together all their possessions and personal effects and bringing them to us so they will be on hand in case they might need to flee and escape. On the steps in the hallway, near the door to our apartment, they sit and lie – women, children and the elderly united in their fear and fate. I was aware of our situation, it is pretty dangerous, yet I was so filled with fear for my mother and my brother that my own personal fate somehow took a second row seat in my mind. Worst of all, I knew that I would now lose any telephone communication with my mother.

At six in the morning the commotion at home began. Everyone began to flee with their belongings. No one knows where to, as long as they are on the move, even without knowing to what direction they flee. We packed our belongings together with Irka. Each of us had two suitcases containing: undergarments, sweaters, socks, a loaf of bread, some flour and sugar and ... 1 liter of vodka in case of emergencies. With such baggage we set out on our journey. We stole through gardens till we reached Leszno Street #191. Off course on the way we had all sorts of adventures and constant automatic gun fire but – that's all just the way it was. On the way we bumped into Lt. Klein's division. They were on their way to the Pawiak Prison,[1] it seems they were on a mission to free the prisoners held there. The Lieutenant smiled widely in our direction and invited us to join their efforts and enlist. "You can be armed female soldiers," he said in short, and continued on his way.

At Leszno Street #191 there was the "Women's Home," where Irka's mother lived. Even under normal circumstances the "Women's Home," is quite a tragic place. So you can imagine how it must look now, that in addition to the prevalent ills such as poverty, hunger, quarrels we now

---

1   Pawiak Prison – Main prison in the Warsaw district, used by the German Security Police and Security Service (SD) from October 1939 to August 1944. Located in Warsaw's Jewish quarter, Pawiak was mainly a prison for men, but it also included a section for women known as "Serbia." It was guarded by SS men and Ukrainian collaborators.

Altogether, some 65,000 prisoners passed through Pawiak, most of whom were Poles from Warsaw. It is unclear how many Jews were interned there. The Jewish prisoners were generally people who had been caught outside the Ghetto. There was also a group of Soviet prisoners of war imprisoned in Pawiak. As a rule, both the Jews and Soviets were shot soon after arriving at the prison. In all, about 32,000 prisoners were shot to death (sometimes in public executions), 23,000 prisoners were transferred to various camps, and several thousand were released. A few prisoners managed to escape from Pawiak, but an attempted revolt against the guards in July 1944 was a failure. Pawiak also had a strong underground that kept in contact with the outside world.

Pawiak, designed to accommodate 1,000 inmates, housed three times that amount, the conditions in the prison were extremely harsh.

One prisoner recalled: "Although a small grated window was open at all times, the air inside the cell was unbearably stuffy – a nasty chill in winter and an equally nagging heat during the summer months. Despite frequent delousing – bedbugs and fleas made inmates lives miserable".

The last transports left Pawiak on July 30, 1944. The remaining prisoners were either released or shot. On August 21, the Germans blew up the prison. (Source: Pawiak 1835 – 1944 – The Guidebook Muzeum Niepodleglosci, Warszawa 2002, Yad VaShem.)

Pawiak Prison.

add fear and panic. This was a fatal addition. The scene which greeted us was as follows: all the contents of the building were gathered in the basement which was used as a bomb shelter. The curator and her daughter, who was herself almost totally senseless in shock and fright due to the great panic around us, Irka's mother, Sophia Vladymirowna (a former Russian aristocrat who was 65 years old) whose bitter fate sent her here, similar to Irka's mother, these are the elite. The rest of the women are dirty and unkempt, sick and women whose murky past is unclear. The majority are destitute beggars and prostitutes. When we arrived we were witnesses to a quarrel which was going on. Someone stole someone else's shoes. Someone cursed someone else. And at the end someone called Irika's mother by the choice epithet [Jew]. (This does not appear in the original diary which was written in hiding.) Since the majority of the women respected and honored Irka's mother – this incident caused quite a stir and tempers flared. Suddenly the curator brought in three injured women with blood running from their faces. I was sure they must have been injured from the shrapnel of a grenade, which was a common site in those days. But how could that have happened? A few minutes later we realized our mistake and we understood what was going on behind the scenes. One of the women who was totally drunk was unable to even stand up straight (it turns out that our stash of vodka meant for emergencies "mysteriously vanished") fell down on her knees before the curator and grasped her hands strongly, kissing each one and murmuring the entire while begging for forgiveness. She was the one who had scratched up the faces of her companions while trying to grab away the open cans of food that they held in their hands. They probably fought with one another for some time and this was evidenced by the blood stained floors. To tell you the truth, this reason behind their injuries was for that period of time strangely odd. However I too understand the meaning of hunger and starvation, especially when it rears its head at such times of uncertainty as these. The incident greatly pained me. I felt the tragedy move me deeply. I wanted to leave these women as fast as possible and as an excuse I took advantage of the rumors that there were Ukrainians not far from us (in the Pawiak Prison) who were wildly rioting in the area, and the rapes and pillaging which resulted. I was surprised that Irka so nonchalantly bid farewell to her mother and left together with me.

Then we began our aimless wanderings, with no final destination – forward. We passed Ogrodowa Street which was full of barricades, we had no choice but to steal past them. From time to time we entered various buildings to rest up a bit. Each time we bumped into the Polish army. These were young men, some armed and some unarmed. They would tell us where we were permitted to go and where we were forbidden. Sometimes they would give us cigarettes or sweets, consoling us with whatever optimistic news the local Polish papers were publicizing that day. When Irka asked me what our final destination was, I warmly squeezed her hand and said: "It does not matter as long as we move on!" We burst out laughing. Really. We had no choice. If it was a choice between either laughter or tears, we chose laughter. Really its the same thing, but it has a certain positive ring to it. It resonates better.

A ten-year-old child told us proudly that he was the liaison and even showed us his A.K. (Armia Krajowa) card. He took us till the office of agriculture, via a short cut which he he expertly and deftly navigated. He succeeded in taking us on a route that was both safe and secure. From there we needed to continue on our own. We entered a church. I sat on the bench and rested my head in my hands, my thoughts concentrating on my mother who was so far away in danger, Mother, my only friend. I started speaking to her, and I began to tell her how badly I was doing, and how difficult it was for me and how lonely I feel. But I believe it will get better, because surely we must be reunited and find each other again.

Suddenly I understood one thing: when I am in a difficult situation, I accept it and my worries for my mother abate somewhat. Before, the thought that everything was okay for me and that she was in such a difficult and precarious situation, troubled me. Now, when my own situation was so much worse I was calmer.

We decided to try and locate Kazik. It was a Utopian fantasy of a dream, but we had no better direction to take, nor any wiser mission to undertake. We remembered had Jasia had once told us that the Armia Ludowa met at the junction where all the Banks intersected at 8 in the morning. We decided to proceed in that direction. From the direction of Ogród Saski Park there came a great explosion and we sat down on the sidewalk of the intersection of the Banks watching and searching for any sight of Kazik. Irka took out a piece of bread from her satchel to nourish herself physically, and she nourished me spiritually by telling me how a few moments before she saw one of Rebellion's newspapers which were being distributed in the streets by the criers, and the paperboy told her that we were expecting sensational news very soon. She has heard top secret information that the army has already reached the city center. I however doubted this fantastic piece of news.

Almost the entire day had passed. We sat there on the sidewalk of the intersection, waiting, but we never succeeded in locating or finding Kazik. Hoping that tomorrow we would find him, we went to seek shelter, to find somewhere to spend the night. The bomb shelter on Senatorska Street 36 became our new home.

8-8-44

Fate led us to this address. There was a great explosion from a bomber that flew overhead above us and we needed to seek shelter in a nearer bomb shelter. To tell you the truth, we did not listen to the rules of safety and security because instead of entering the shelter we stood at that entrance of the building, watching where the bombs fell. It was an interesting game, as crazy as it sounds, a game of nerves asking, "is this bomb meant for me or a bit further off?"

We were witness to massive explosion of bombs which fell in the neighborhoods of "Żelazną Bramą" and "Hala Mirowska." We found ourselves only a few hundred meters from there. The commander of the anti-aircraft forces Col. Kujawa, who we coincidentally recognized during the bombings, was very gracious towards us. When he learned about our bitter fate he invited us warmly into the shelter.

Until now, in this shelter, we became an attraction, the first frightened pigeons (later on the shelter would fill up with those rescued from bombings). The residents of the building did their best to make us feel at home and offered us their help. We did not know whose invitations for lunch and dinner to accept and from whom we should borrow extra undergarments and linens. The officer visited us from time to time and checked up on us, asking us if we lacked anything. He brought us canned food even liqueur and champagne, however we refused the latter so as to prevent our relationship from becoming more intimate. Even Ms. Kowlaska, a strange old maid who never married, showered us with warmth and accepted us into her home as if we were her own daughters. It seems that in such terrible times the good inclination comes to the fore and not just the evil side of people. Ms. Kowalska cooked, laundered and even worried over us. She slept near us in the shelter so as to prevent the comings on of several men who showed us too much affection including trying to cover us at night with blankets.

Today passed quietly. We took a tour of the shelter which houses some one thousand residents in all. There are quite a few injured people, transferred from the Maltański hospital which is not far from here. In our hall which is about 40 meters in size, there are as many people as there are meters so that there was no air circulation. The worst was that the air vents were covered by sand bags. The lack of ventilation was unbearable. The injured suffered especially badly. We tried to spend as little time as possible in the shelter and we also asked of the other residents to do as we did, yet it did not help matters much. The air was stale and heavy and this made the injured weaker and sicker.

9-8-44

We slept wonderfully, all the inhabitants took care to make us comfortable. Our luxury beds were actually cardboard boxes (because the building used to house the Meiner winery) we even had pillows and blankets. In the morning we had an important visitor in the form of Col. Kujawa. Since we realized that he was quite smart, just and intelligent we seized the opportunity to engage him in a serious conversation regarding our political situation. We were interested in hearing his approach to the topic. This was the first time that I heard the cruel truth: "We must be prepared for the fact that only swift outside intervention can save us" – he declared, "*Porywać się z motyką na słońce* (Literal translation: To lunge at the sun with a hoe.) They have bitten off more than they can chew!" – "Those are just romantic fantasies typical of our Polish mindset," – he retorted, "have you taken a good look at our army? It is true that the majority are young twenty-year-olds, full of energy, hope and courage, however these are the youth who live in the clouds. True seasoned men, realistic full of life's experience, these we are sorely lacking. This uprising is unruly, unplanned, and the Soviet army is but thirty kilometers away from the Vistula river and is no rush at all to enter Warsaw. They are waiting for us to do battle to the last drop of Polish blood. The antagonism appearing in the uprising's papers by our own press regarding the red army is a grave error, it makes matters worse and compromises our position. The strained relations between the Armia Krajowa and the Armia Ludowa is splitting our own nation in half. The help we are dreaming of receiving from the English army is a fantasy. They shall limit themselves to invading with dolls (during the first days of the uprising the English planes made one flight over Warsaw and parachuted dolls down). This was simply a trick to surprise and scare the Germans. The Polish rebels were sorely disappointed. I am emphasizing once more that we will never succeed in our objectives on our own without outside help." I am sad that he is right. Irka is depressed by the conversation. I try to console her, but I myself am not convinced either.

In the early morning hours we showed up at Maltański hospital as volunteer nurses. We need to keep ourselves busy. To our chagrin the hospital was full to overflowing with volunteers so that there was no room for us. We are trying to make ourselves useful in some way. Instead we helped by organizing a new branch for the hospital in the building where we were staying on the first and second floors. We needed to move the injured and it was very difficult work. I will describe just one scene: We are moving an injured man from the underground shelter to the first floor, suddenly the siren catches us by surprise half way. Common sense tells us to turn back and head to the shelter however that simply cannot be done because of the panic that ensues around us. People are running in sheer terror towards the shelter and barely even notice us. Each push causes the injured man terrible pain and we must stand waiting so as to not block the way. In a weak whisper the injured man asks us to leave him and seek shelter but our conscience forbids us to do so, despite the great fear. Above us there is the loud din of roaring German aircraft. We remain by the side of the injured man. After several minutes have passed and the way has cleared since everyone is in the shelter we quietly transfer the injured patient as well.

When we exited the shelter we saw a young group of men dressed in prisoner's uniforms. They were working at collecting and transporting waste and garbage and they told us the following story: When the rebels conquered the Pawiak prison there were three hundred fifty prisoners released who had been sentenced to death. Is that not a miracle? A wave of boundless happiness washed over us when we heard. For me this was one of the nicest things that occurred during the time of the uprising.

Those prisoners which I met near the Maltański hospital were saved but not connected to these others.

Two months have before the uprising and rebellion began, the Germans began to empty the city of any and all valuables. Twenty former prisoners were employed in the transport of liquor and alcoholic beverages from the Meindel company's store rooms on Senatorska Street 36. When the situation in Warsaw worsened to the point where they fled in panic the Germans locked them all in the cellar and basically sentenced them to death by starvation. Thanks to Col. Kujawa, who happened to pass by and hear the sounds of their knocking on the doors of their prison, these prisoners received their freedom and merited to once again see the light of day. I noticed that the attitude of the Poles towards these prisoners was a mix of mercy and arrogance. Although there is no shame in work, whatever form it may be, the degrading type of work they had placed upon them really got my blood boiling. To me the conduct of the Poles resembled as if they had simply inherited their conduct from the Germans the feelings of a master race against the weak and lowly inferior races. Now the former German slave workers became slaves to the Poles instead. One of the prisoners, a Greek, old, weak and with a frightened look on his face awakened feelings of mercy in me to such a degree that without thinking twice I handed him the only loaf of bread we had. Irka pierced me with a look of pure astonishment, although she did not actually oppose my actions. Surely she hoped we would at least have split the loaf between us. I tried to quickly console her by saying that surely by doing a good deed we would be rewarded[2] and that if we had been so far saved from death by a bullet surely we would not die of starvation either. However my gift of bread caused quite a stir: One of the younger Greeks, whose name was Kovo, a witness to our handing of the loaf to his fellow former prisoner, attacked him in a language we could not understand and tried to grab the loaf of bread away from him. At first I thought that the young man also wanted a piece of the bread, however his true intention was immediately apparent. It was his pride

---

2   Translator's note: Compare this scenario to the Talmudic story in Tractate Bava Metzia 62a where Ben Petura says that if two men were in the desert, and one has a flask of just enough water to enable only one of them to return to civilization, but if they share it, both will die, it is best that they share the water, and neither will see the other die. However R. Akiva derives from the verse: "*Ve'Chei Achicha Imach* – Your brother will live with you" – that your own life takes precedence over another's life.

that caused his reaction, not withstanding the years of being put down, his sense of dignity and human self worth remained. He argued that, we were all in the same situation now and therefore all of equal standing, therefore the bread belonged to us and that in a situation such as ours it is wrong to try and give charity. At the moment we connected through a mutual understanding of each other.

Late in the evening we ventured out to the courtyard to get some fresh air to breathe before spending the night in the stuffy underground shelter. Irka sat on a broken crate and I lay beside her. We sat meditating on our fate. Suddenly our gazes fell on the shadow of a man who stood facing the wall as his entire body swayed and shook back and forth in a strange manner. In the almost total darkness, it was hard to make out what he was doing. After several minutes understanding dawned upon me: this is a Jew and he is praying Ma'ariv, the evening prayers. His prayers continued and we too sat there silently in the dark, excited and mesmerized by the scene, trying to remain quiet not to profane such a lofty moment. I whispered to Irka: "This prayer is known as the shemone esrei." I remembered from my grandfather's home that it was prayed three times a day while standing, once in the morning, once in the afternoon and once after sundown. It contains eighteen blessings hence its Hebrew name. Irka suggested we ask him if he indeed was reciting this prayer and thereby he would realize that we were co-religionists of his. We approached him and asked "Shemone Esrei?" He nodded his head in agreement and raised his hands up in supplication to G-d and blessed us. For us this blessing was a sure sign that we would be protected and that we would survive the war peacefully.

10-8-44

As the hour nears eight in the morning Irka reminds us once again about the meetings of the Armia Ludowa at the bank's intersection. We decided once more to search for Kazik. There is a heavy rain of bullets from the direction of Krasinski park.

We steal towards Rymarska street, and do our best to cling to the walls of the building. Irka encourages me by saying that my white shirt camouflages with the walls of the buildings so that I will be hidden from the enemy. We had great Mazal. A moment after we passed the Germans fired a hail of bullets in our direction and we could see the bullet holes in the walls which shared my shirt color ... it seems to be a bit crazy – the way we did not even think of that. But sometimes during war insanity takes over and succeeds where what was well thought out and the best laid plans and schemes would have failed. We wait for Kazik suspensefully. The car used as a makeshift ambulance, carrying the sick and injured has passed by us several times already, on its way to Maltanski hospital. The nurse stands in the car waving a white flag with the emblem of the Red Cross. She warns us with her finger of the danger we are in. I know that it matters to Irka very much that we find Kazik and therefore despite my misgivings we continue to wait. Only after several hours have passed do we decide to leave. We return sad and disappointed. The weather is wonderful, the sun is shining but inside, in our souls everything is cold, dead and frozen solid. What disharmony! We continue once again to roam around hopelessly. I try to cheer Irka up a bit, and I convince her that we should collect some potatoes from the nearby fields around us. In normal times such an act would be considered theft, but now it is an act of bravery, because above us fly the enemy's planes.

When we approach nearer to the shelter at 36 Senatorska Street we notice smoke rising from the windows of the cellar. Our home is on fire! We run in the direction of the flames. When we reach the stairs we are met by nurses transporting the injured from the cellar. We grab onto a stretcher and help. Only after several moments do we take in the scene around us and understand the situation. The Germans have penetrated and invaded our territory, they are throwing grenades into the cellars and forcing the civilian population outdoors into the streets.

We are in the courtyard. Suddenly, I felt a sharp blow on my back. I turned my head and before my eyes stands a German soldier stabbing me with the bayonet of his rifle and motioning me to descend with him into the cellar to find those that are in hiding. He tells me to warn them that the Germans intend to set all the surrounding buildings and homes on fire so that all the people must be evacuated. I march down the dark hallway, choking on smoke and calling out loud: "Everyone must leave the cellar, the house is on fire."

It turns out that the cellar was completely empty. The choking smoke chased everyone out of their hiding places. When the German soldier realized that we were alone he set himself on me and roared in anger: "I have just returned from Russia and I have not seen a woman in months." He tried to throw me to the ground. I fought him with all my strength. The darkness became my ally because his blows missed me several times. At some point I managed to free myself and get away from him and escape. I ran forward without paying any attention to the direction I ran. The German soldier was screaming: "I am firing!" But he did not fire, it seems, that it was thanks to darkness and choking smoke.

I reached the first floor and another miracle occurred. The doors of the elevator stood open before me. I ran into the elevator, closed the doors, pressed the button and began to ascend. I do not know whether I lost consciousness in the elevator or whether I fell asleep. All I do know is that when I finally exited the elevator it was night time. Slowly, slowly I crept towards the courtyard. It was empty and deserted. I continued moving forward, looking right and left, but everything is deserted. Where is Irka? I continue towards the neighboring building, searching. From afar I see a small group of people. Each one is equipped with two pails of water, and using the most primitive means at their disposal they are trying to put out the fire by running to and from the water to the fire and back again. As I drew near I hoped I would find Irka. Someone exhausted from the task passed on his pails to me and asked me to take his place. I take the pails and join the group. We work fast, running with our pails to and fro, continuing the cycle again and again without a break. There is not even a moment's gap to brush the sweat from our foreheads, we are a small group and the fire is growing stronger. After superhuman efforts, during which I cannot even count the hours, we succeeded in putting out the fire. Only then did I truly realize the fact that I had lost Irka. She was probably evacuated with the rest of the inhabitants. Someone whispers that he witnessed them lined up by the Germans as a human barrier against the oncoming tanks! Was Irka among them? It is very difficult for me to accept that thought. During war, I guess, the most painful moments are when you depart and bid farewell to those that are closest to you. The blows I received from the German soldier did not pain me as much as these thoughts.

I sat down on a stone, laid back against the wall and cried. However that is how life is, one problem is solved and a new one crops up. In a moment I found myself in new trouble. I problem which is difficult to solve. My pocketbook containing all my worldly possessions and especially my documents vanished. I do not know exactly when it happened or under what circumstances. Maybe I lost it when I ran from the cellar. Maybe I left it in the elevator. I cannot return to those locations and I know the danger that awaits me. Losing my personal documents means losing my right to life. Without them I became myself once more. And to be me, to have my own identity – was forbidden to me. For people like myself the concentration camps are waiting. I think of Ludwig. At what efforts he invested to procure Aryan documents for me. "I will think of this tomorrow," Scarlet O'Hara says to herself in the book "Gone with the Wind", and this is how I too, solved my own dilemma.

11-8-44

I am so lonely, this alone pushes me to write. It is hard to imagine after everything that happened to me today that I am still capable of taking my pen in hand and to concentrate on writing. If loneliness is macabre, maybe writing will give me some false feeling of connection to those that I love and care about, to those who I yearn to speak to and tell my tale.

Maybe these lone pages will somehow reach them one day and from these pages they will know that at the most difficult moments in my life my thoughts, feelings and emotions were with them.

This daily entry in my diary I wish to dedicate to Mietek (Mietek Kowalski a worker, a leftist, his whereabouts are unknown), he is an ordinary citizen who you can pass by without noticing. I met Mietek during the darkness in the shelter. I felt his presence beside me, more than I could see him.

After we put out the fire a small group of six of us remained: the Pollaks – a father, mother and two older children, Mietek and I. Nightfall came and we needed to think of how to find something to eat, our first meal that day altogether, and here to spend the night. The Pollaks who lived in that building had a better situation. They succeeded in getting up into their apartment on the first floor and to find some food. They brought some bread, cold soup and some onions with them to the shelter. It was a treasure. I sat alone in the cellar, in a corner lost in my thoughts. Mrs. Pollak took care of her husband and her children. She prepared a place for them to sleep and gave out food to them. She offered me also, a piece of bread and some soup, however I could not take it, even though a hungry person should never refuse. My throat however, was clamped shut. Now, I have to admit, that although it seems silly, and even childishly out of place, my greatest problem was jealousy. Not giving up on a hopeless situation, not fear of tomorrow, not terror from what the night might bring, and not the pestering hunger; just a simple human weakness – jealousy; it ate me up. I could not stand to see how the Pollaks cared for each other. How close they were to one another, and how the mother kissed and hugged her daughter. It was unbearable for me.

In the darkness I felt Mietek. He was alone like me. I approached him and said to him, "Do you see sir, next to us there is a family and they belong to each other. I too would like to have someone near and dear to me. Can we be together?" Mietek answered, "Okay." I suggested that we ascend to search the apartments, perhaps we would find some scraps of food. He answered me curtly, "You stay here in the shelter and I will worry about it." My heart felt good. First of all that he said to me, using the informal "you" and not the formal "miss" which made me feel closer to him. And secondly, it made me feel that here was someone who worried and cared about me. I had not recognized, nor felt that feeling for weeks. After several minutes Mietek returned with some booty: He had procured dry black bread, some potatoes, some cream and wine. What a feast! We drank some wine and our moods brightened. I told him of how I escaped, about the elevator, and he grew excitedly agitated when he heard about my lost documents. "You will be in trouble because of this. These days someone without papers and documents ... Anyone who asks you to identify yourself and you won't have any means to do so, will draw conclusions and grow suspicious. If they are Germans, they will be suspicious of your background, that you are Jewish. If they will be Poles, they will be suspicious that you are a spy. I am sorry to say the only solution will be to tell them that you are my wife." I answered him, "If you agree, then I will be your wife." Mietek revealed himself to be one the purest individuals I have ever met in my entire life.

14-8-44

At five in the morning we decided to go on our way. Our final destination was the Old City. Because Mietek had once worked in the Mandel factory he knew the area where there were storage rooms well, and using side routes and less traveled ways we succeeded making our way past the Maltanski hospital, and behind it we found a hiding place beneath large cartons and we remained there till evening. In the evening we stole without being identified by the German patrol towards the Old City. We ran forward without knowing the way well and a miracle occurred, the Armia Krajowa's patrol stopped us and one of the soldiers on patrol was – none other than – what a strange coincidence – Mietek's brother! They asked me for my identification. I looked towards Mietek despondently and he answers bravely, "She is my wife." Mietek's brother – Michael – cannot believe his own ears: "Mietek, when did this happen? You got married? You the sworn bachelor! The master of your own principles?!" Michael falls upon me with affection saying: "You could not have found a better young man. Mietek is a golden boy!" Michael gives us an update on what is going on in the Old City. He is a typical

Armia Krajowa soldier, he says everything rose-colored. "Our boys will show them. We are hitting the Germans as hard as we can. The Old City will always serve as our symbol of the courage, bravery and strength of the Polish people. The Polish soldier is the best soldier there is." etc etc blah blah blah. I gave Mietek a look. He seems about to respond but in the end he holds back. He changes the subject and asks for directions to the address of acquaintances, the Yanitzskis, who live on Starówka (in the Old City). We have our first real destination.

Despite the explosions and the mortars that we nicknamed cows, because of their sound similar to the mooing of a cow, we met up with the Janickis in their apartment and not in their cellar. They greeted us warmly and affectionately, blessed Mietek admiring his lovely "wife" and complained about the lack of food and water. During the modest meal an argument broke out over the state of the rebellion, that was the first time that I learned Mietek's position on the matter, which to me seemed quite realistic. He saw the rebellion as a romantic movement by the youth, lacking any basic plan or foundation and destined to failure. He explained that the commander General Bor, wants to prove to the world that the Poles do not want and do not need the help and intervention of the Red Army in order to defeat the Germans. They wish to establish an independent free Polish government here in Warsaw. The temporary government which has been established in Lublin is for them, the potential victors, a foreign body with which we will have to come to terms with over time. Mietek was very agitated. He did not even taste the food, complaining of a stomachache. The next day we heard the same complaints and once again he ate nothing all day. Before evening, Michael made a surprise appearance with a large arsenal of food: two loaves of bread, sugar and potatoes. Michael laid down the package, proud of the bounty and invited us to partake of a festive meal. Suddenly I saw that Mietek was happy and joyful, his eyes shone as he broke the bread and cut the loaves, distributing them among us. He gobbled up his own portion with gusto. I reminded him "Mietek, this is fresh bread and you are complaining of stomach pains." He whispered into my ear: "I was just pretending. I simply did not want to be a burden on the Janickis. You saw how the food shortage troubled them." At that moment I realized that Mietek had fasted because of me. In order that I accept his self sacrifice he simply pretended to me. I was simultaneously touched and horrified at his wondrous actions. Then I understood that I too, was being a burden on him. I resolved to release him of his need to worry for me. I suggested that I volunteer my services to the army as a nurse. He accepted my proposal however he added, "Do as you wish, I myself will never be drafted to serve on this army."

18-8-44

The Kościół Garnizonowy church served as a military garrison and command center. I approached and volunteered my services. They did not ask me for any documents. They looked at me scrutinizingly and declared that I must take on a fictitious name and "you look Jewish, we recommend the name Yuditka." My heart began to pound furiously, but on the outside I put on a smile and barely forced out the few words "That name sounds good to me; it sounds different, Yuditka!" At that moment I realized just how much danger my Semitic appearance had put me in, despite my Aryan documents. Luckily, the Germans were not as good as the Poles in identifying Jews.

They showed me where I would sleep on the floor. I received two blankets and food rations. They sent me to the doctor, Dr. Kristina, who I was to work together with, caring for the injured. I did not even have a chance to place my things into my little corner nor did I even have the chance to get to know my new boss – immediately I began to hear orders barked at me fast and furiously: "Hand me cotton bandages, they are on the left in the drawer! Bring me injections and syringes! Fill the syringe!"

A moment ago they had brought in an injured ten-year-old boy who needed our care. I tried to follow the orders as fast as possible. My hands shook and the minute I accomplished all the tasks, syringe in hand, a weariness washed over me as I saw the bleeding child. I pushed the syringe into Dr. Kristina's hand and fainted. Two soldiers carried me into the courtyard where I awoke and revived. I was embarrassed at how "well" I began my career as a nurse.

Three more times the same scenario repeated itself. I would give first aid to an injured man, and at the last moment once his wounds were bandaged, then I fainted. Obviously this caused me to be the object of mockery for the soldiers. The second time I was called to administer first aid the soldiers grabbed the nearest stretcher and filed in line, following behind me, demonstrating how prepared they were for my next fainting spell, to carry me out on the stretcher.

To my disappointment I had to give up my position as volunteer nurse because my sensitivity to the sight of blood was simply too much. I must have inherited the trait from my father. I remember how he once told me that he was unable to enter a hospital because he would faint at the smell of medicine. I was very depressed because of this shortcoming. They suggested that instead I become a liaison officer and I agreed. The night was simply horrible. The artillery shelling continued nonstop. All the young men of our division went out for an exercise and all the mattresses remained unoccupied. They did not want to enlist any of the women because of the great danger involved. Each one of the young soldiers left in a different mood: Some left willingly and happily, however some others, especially those for whom this was their first nighttime exercise, saw the specter of death before their eyes, they left in a serious mood. They were lost in thought, and genuflected, crossing themselves before they left. We three liaison officers were the only ones left. All night long we waited in terror for their return. The division returned before dawn, they were three less soldiers.

Zanto and Domb, two inseparably friends, always together. This time fate separated them, Zanto returned and came back to us, however Domb was shot in the stomach and was taken to a field hospital. The young men were silent about the exercise. They were depressed. Three wounded was a very high number for such a small group of thirty soldiers in all. In the morning we ran under a downpour of enemy fire, and as it rained bullets we made our way to the field hospital.

The field hospital is overflowing. Hundreds of injured soldiers in severe and critical condition lie on the floor. There is a shortage of dressings and whites, a shortage of food and medical supplies. No one records the names of the injured. There is no way I can locate the injured from our own division. From every direction come sighs and cries for help. I feel myself about to faint once more. I try with all my might to hold myself up. I pinch myself with my nails, but that doesn't help either. Again I was taken out on a stretcher.

Wanda found Domb, he is in critical condition. We return to the command center. The morale of the soldiers is low. I hear horror stories about what the soldiers endured, but I do not have the strength to retell them. I am told that my acquaintance from Lwów, Ludwig Ridler, fell at a barricade. A mortar shell hit him head on and blew him into pieces, to the point where the friend who stood beside him a moment ago saw him vanish. How can we withstand this? We are giving up hope like paralytics. Even us liaison officers have no job left to do.

28-8-44

I have not written now for several days. It's a shame, because if I do not make it out of here, this [diary] will serve as my only witness of what has happened to me. Maybe it [this diary] has a greater chance than I do of making it to my relatives.

We are enduring hell on earth. Days on end we care for the wounded. Each hour their numbers increase at a terrifying rate. The greatest tragedy is the lack of anesthetics. All surgery is performed with the patients awake and conscious. After such difficult days we collapse spent and exhausted unto our beds. I am incapable of and I do not wish to force myself to repeat the horrible scenes which I went through during those days, to pass before my eyes those visions of horror, I would rather erase them and blot them out of my memory.

I must add only one thing: I no longer pass out and faint at the sight of an injured person. What I have gone through has strengthened me. The songs of the rebellion which we used to sing at night sounds sadder day by day. The song of "G-d in heaven, return our home to us."

30-8-44

Next to the church there is a first aid station. Only one thought constantly wracks my mind: I must break into there and find poison. I know that many of the rebels carry cyanide. Only I have none. Why? It can be the greatest freedom from my current situation. Even though I am naturally optimistic, the fact is that the Old City is in its death throes. There is no help arriving from anywhere. We are surrounded from all sides by the German enemy forces. There is no hope of escaping this blockade.

I am at the first aid station, searching excitedly for poison. Through the glass doors of the medicine cabinet I spot a bottle with the picture of a skull on it. How will I get it? I lean my head against the glass and the thoughts begin to whirl around in my head ... this is the first time in my life that I stand facing death – unafraid. In my thoughts I say goodbye to my mother and to my brother Juleck. I speak only to them. Suddenly something strange happens to me. A strong force pierces me with faith in the coming world of the afterlife. Calm. Serenity. And I feel as though I will once again meet with my father, Ludwik, and with my beloved Uncle Arthur. It is such a wonderful feeling, I feel at peace with my decision to leave.

But I did not "leave." What made me return to the present was a loud noise. I thought the entire building would collapse. It turns out that our forces downed a German warplane and it crashed directly into the roof of the adjoining building. Everyone runs to see the charcoaled body of the pilot shouting "Hooray!" It raised everyone's morale, but mine.

However I did get out of the mood that I was in previously. I returned to my division. I helped prepare dinner for the soldiers and I went to sleep. The night was peaceful, as if everything slept in silence.

1-9-44

Zonta told me today: "Do not take what is happening to us to heart. That is why there is a central command. For a soldier is forbidden to think [on his own]." Since I am but a simple soldier, I am ready to follow any order. To my dismay no actions are taken to try and save the remnants of our army. Someone invoked the name: "Westerplatte."[3]

2-9-44

At night we tried to break through Krasinski Park. The exercise failed and we retreated broken in body and spirit. All night long we were under a rain of enemy gunfire and bullets. We have so many injured. Towards the morning I fell asleep on the stairs of the archives. The sounds of mooing "cows" awoke me. We ran to the cellar to take shelter. What will be from here on?

The Kościół Garnizonowy church, where our division is stationed is under great stress and suspense. Rumors reached me that our forces are fleeing the Old City. Sadly and emotionally each one of us rounds up their modest belongings including a few personal effects and some food. We have yet to receive any orders. We are simply getting ourselves ready. Based on the rumors in the field, it will happen today, through the sewers and for the army alone.

I decided to try and locate Mietek as fast as possible. To say goodbye and to thank him for what he had done for me. I hoped that he would

---

3   Westerplatte, where the first shots of World War II were fired on September 1, 1939, is a fort near Danzig. It was the scene of a fierce battle in September 1939, where a Polish garrison held off numerically superior German troops for several days. Finally, the Westerplatte garrison, who were now exhausted with many defenders severely wounded, as well as being short on food, water, ammunition and medical supplies, surrendered on September 7, 1939. It became a symbol of Polish heroism and courage.

Hale Mirowskie (Mirów's Halls, formerly Trade or Marketplace Halls – Hale Targowe) are trade centers (halls) constructed in 1899-1901 in Mirów district in Warsaw. Until their destruction during Warsaw Uprising in 1944 they were the largest trade centers in Warsaw. They were rebuilt in the period of 1950s-1960s and restored to their original function as trade centers.

*Krasinski
Park.*

*Krasinski Square –
sewers entrance.*

*Krasinski
Palace.*

agree to join our division and leave the Old City together with us. I should explain that due to Mietek's political opinions he was not willing to serve in the Armia Krajowa. Since I did not know the date and time when we would take action and move, I was afraid to leave my friends, lose all hope of communications with them and to bid them farewell. However my feelings for Mietek and my desire to find him were greater.

I ran to the Janicki family's apartment. But I found it deserted. I was not surprised because many people left their apartments, spending most of the hours of the day hiding in the cellars and shelters. I checked the shelters in the area, one by one. I asked passersby, but I was unsuccessful. Sad and disappointed, I went back to the church, but in my heart I hoped that we would meet once again.

Lost in thought, I awoke from my reverie only when Lt. Sigmund grabbed me by the arm and yelled at me: "Where did you vanish to? Are you normal? We were searching for you for over an hour already! In a few minutes we are heading towards the center of town through the sewers." I take my bag and without a word, I follow Sigmund. He leads me to the opening of a sewer grate at the intersection of the banks. There we found a long line of soldiers in camouflaged uniforms. These uniforms were captured from the Germans and became the rebels'.

I am too far away from the opening of the sewer and so I await my turn to descend. My thoughts turn once again to my mother and Juleck. Will I find them at the other end of the tunnel? Will I ever succeed in meeting them again?

I am familiar with this painful route from an earlier, failed exercise. Then we also used the sewers heading in the direction of Mokotow. That time we had to turn back. The Germans dropped grenades down the open manholes. But actually that itself was not the reason we turned back and retreated. It was our luck that there were no casualties. When they raised the dam and the floodgates opened, the water level began to steadily rise and we were in danger of being swept away by the strong current, and we were in danger of drowning in that putrid water. Since I was the last in line, the water reached my knees; however those who decided to retreat were at the head of the line – there the water reached up to their necks. This time I am not pessimistic and I believe in my good fortune.

I have but one small wish in my heart and that is to remain in line near Lt. Sigmund. It is very prosaic, since Lt. Sigmund has a bottle of vodka and I know that at difficult times a few sips of vodka can distance you from feelings of danger.

As the time drags on and the long line moves slowly suddenly I hear a voice call out "Yuditka!" I turn around and a funny sight greets me. One of the fellows in the Parsol division is headed my way, his steps are uncharacteristically light and giddy. He skips and dances towards me and presents me with gifts: an expensive fur, an exquisite powder box and a cigarette case engraved with the initials K. Z. I stare at the gifts in wonder, uncomprehendingly. Seeing my bafflement he explains. It seems that the Old City streets are filled with expensive objects of all kinds, strewn about by fleeing residents on the run. Anything you want can be found. But in such a situation as I am in, who wants anything anyway? I only keep for myself the cigarette case, holding onto it like a talisman to ward off evil.

In the end I stand at the mouth of the manhole. I descend, aided by the round-bellied metal bars. At the last moment I take one last sweeping look searching sadly for Mietek. My eyes fill with tears. I hide them because "a soldier does not cry." Minutes tick by and I find myself swallowed up by the darkness of the underground tunnels. Now I can finally cry. We march on slowly and silently, sloshing through the putrid waters in the tunnel. It is so dark that I cannot even make out the form of the soldier marching in front of me. I feel no fear; just a strange apathy, maybe because the way is so long and monotonous. I close my eyes to avoid seeing the darkness (what a paradox!). Even the stench of the sewer no longer bothers me. We march on, and nothing happens, marching and thinking. We do not exchange a word between ourselves. We fear that the Germans might hear us through the manholes above us. We fear that the moment they discover us, they will begin throwing down grenades through the openings. A deathly silence hangs over us, the only sound is the rush of the waters beneath our feet.

We have reached our destination. After about an hour and a half or so of wandering, we see daylight. The manhole opening to Śródmieście is open. We are on Wilcza Street. A unit comprised of a doctor, a nurse and several soldiers is waiting for us. They distribute food, water and record our names. I approach the registration booth and I am to register myself under my name and I cannot say a word.

Which name should I give? Who am I now? How much can I reveal openly about myself to these people?

Although they are Poles and there are no Germans among them, are these my people? Can I reveal my true identity?

Names spin around in my head: Gruenfeld, Heibowicze, Skrybayło but the name which is most well engraved in my mind is Yuditka –

Jewess, the name I was given by my own division to which I belonged. I was scared to admit who I really and truly was, because I heard once in a while their conversations filled with venom and hatred towards Jews. I accepted the odd pseudonym with a wide grin.

"My dear, we are asking for your name!" But I was silent. "Leave her, she is suffering from shock."

3-9-44

Dressed in my spotted camouflage army uniform, my face is caked with dried dust and sewer water like makeup. The dried mud forms a grotesque mask on my face.

I reach 56 Ulica Mokotowska. There, in the underground shelter, I found my mother and Juleck. They did not even recognize me.

Ludwig Zelig – A Memoir

L wów, Poland: The year is 1939, and Lwów is under the rule of the Union of Soviet Socialist Republics (U.S.S.R.). We are still managing to live in the same city and in our very same home. Yet somehow as much as things are the same, everything has changed; somehow everything is different. The people are the same, but they have changed. Not everyone, but those that have not changed are silent, distrustful and do not believe in their fellows. They have retreated inside themselves. They weigh carefully each spoken word; each sentence uttered is scrutinized because one can never know who is standing somewhere nearby, listening.

Ludwig

The populace and citizens have divided into several different groups. One group is the Communists. Many of these members once sat in prison or were persecuted by the Polish government and now they have become society's elite ruling class. Another group is the "new Communists," those who are looking for upward mobility and a career (like the nouveau riche); they chase after new positions. The third group is the unaffiliated, those who lack a social ideology. What matters to them is only what past social position they once held and what their former positions in society were. They are all living in constant fear and terror that they will be either incarcerated or deported to Siberia according to the notorious section 11 laws.

The Polish patriots are the last group who have formed the underground. Ludwig and I represent two disparate groups. He chose

Poland as his motherland, although he was Jewish. Ludwig aligned himself with the typical youthful romantic patriotism so characteristic of Polish youth during those times. I, who was raised in a Jewish home with Jewish and Zionistic values, was far from the spirit of assimilation. We were both students in the Gymnasium.

It all started in History class. The air was full of strain and palatable tension. Our professor, Dr. Kleighoffer, told us with tears in her eyes that one of our own classmates had informed on her to the political commissar, an official of the Communist Party who was assigned to teach party principles to our school. They had given testimony that she was teaching false historical facts to us. The slander of our professor created an unbearable situation for us. The school year had just begun a month ago and we still lacked proper books and study materials for history, based on the new rules set down by the new ruling Communist Party, which wanted us to study from material which followed its Communist world view.

Our new principals felt that whatever we had learned previously was twisted and crooked, false and the fruit of the corrupt Capitalists. Dr. Kleighoffer was now forced to correcting the "false" materials we had been learning and changing facts, such as calling the *eliantim* our enemies and portraying our (former) enemies as our new friends and collaborators. Everything she taught became mixed up completely, and as her students, we could tell that her teaching career would soon reach its end. She had lost any authority or credibility she had had with us.

As fate smiled on me, in this class of all classes, I received a note, crumpled up into a paper ball. I opened the note and could barely read the illegible scribbles there that said, "If you wish to join us in a protest before the coming Polish Independence Day on November 11, approach Ludwig Zelig on Raytheon Street 1." I was not interested so much in attending the protest as I was in meeting Ludwig, of whom I had already heard some interesting things. He was known as an interesting personality, an artist, a poet and generally someone who drew attention to himself, someone people noticed. I reached Raytheon Street approximately a quarter of an hour before the time that the demonstration was to take place in hopes that I would find Ludwig alone, so that I could explain to him why I could not take part. This of course was a sham of an excuse I had made up for myself.

Ludwig was living by that time on his own. As I had heard, in his apartment clandestine meetings took place where the Polish youth gathered to fight against the Soviet regime. The apartment was very modest but well kept and neat. It reminded me more of a craftsman's workroom than living quarters. The large table propped against the wall was full of carpenter's tools, brushes and paints. And propped up on the stand stood – at first I could not believe my eyes – a portrait of me done in charcoal, based on the photo of my student ID. Ludwig saw my surprise. Surely he anticipated the reaction, and immediately he explained himself: These are four from Hungary, two from Palestine, Madagascar and Alaska. I was totally bewildered and had no idea what he was talking about, but he immediately cleared it up by adding: "That is the amount of postage stamps that your younger brother Juleck had me trade him for your photo."

I was proud that I, that is my photo, was held in such high esteem by Ludwig. This was a Platonic relationship, something of the past, but I must write my memoirs as they are accepted today.

Ludwig had a special personality which drew many to him. He had a natural charisma and personal charm. He was fragile of spirit, yet full of understanding and dedication to others. He was handsome, not too tall, blond-haired and greenish-blue-eyed. His personality was somewhat of a mystery. He had the soul of a poet. Maybe in his poetry he revealed more of himself.

On November 11, 1939, Polish Independence Day, he marched together with the Polish youth on the streets of Lwów and sang the Polish national anthem. He carried a sign which read "Poland shall continue."

I stood all worried on the side praying for his safety. I was scared that his youthful enthusiasm might lead him to a tragic end. I did not participate in the march, but in my heart, I was with them.

That day Ludwig did not come home. They searched for him late into night with no success. On the next day, his father received the news that his son had been charged with counter-revolutionary activities and that he was incarcerated at the police station. Thanks to some convincing, in the form of bribery, the police were persuaded to release Ludwig and he was set free. It is unclear what the terms of his release were, but it seems likely that the handsome sum of money that was donated to their cause did the trick. From that moment on, the young patriots changed course and their activities took on a new form. They went underground and their meetings became even more secretive. Their goal was to encourage the spirit of Polish nationalism. They studied and recited Polish poetry, sang Polish national songs and tried to strengthen their love for their homeland. These meetings led to the birth of literature and prose on the subject of Poland's having been conquered. At these times Ludwig's prose was heard.

In the year 1941, the Germans entered Lwów. The regime changed hands, but the underground movement continued its activities. Their work was different. It had taken on a more hands on, a more real nature. It had a real purpose. Ludwig and several friends began to forge documents and falsify identity papers.

The cellar on Raytheon Street gave birth to a lab where "new people" with "new identities" were created and born. Names, birthdates, nationalities, birthplaces – all were changed and swapped at will. Only faces remained the same, glued to their ID cards and documents. An artistic element was needed to color and touch up some of these photos. Ludwig became a source for forged Aryan documents for those that sought them. He guided the bearers and offered them information on where to go and with whom they should meet and contact in other cities. He, himself never left Lwów. He continued his blessed work and did not join those that he saved.

In July of 1943, he reached the end of his days. He was taken just as many other anonymous brave and courageous were as well. The chain of endless struggle was severed and cut, the young lofty soul was snuffed out. His poems he left behind as a testimony, as words of thanksgiving to those he helped save and to those who survived and lived on. Perhaps they did so, thanks to his encouragement and strength which he gave them as he worked so courageously, with great power of spirit, always ready to suffer and sacrifice himself for others.

May his memory be blessed.

Destiny, Coincidence Or Higher Power?

The year is 2011. I am visiting my son Eli in the beautiful Galilean city of Karmiel. We are together with Eli's wife, Michal, and their children, Eyal, Tal and Lilach. It is my granddaughter Lilach's birthday and we are all celebrating the occasion together. Only my daughter Maya and her family are missing. She cannot be with us since she is living in Los Angeles, California. Arik, who is married to Yamit, has a two-year-old daughter Shaili, and Asaf the younger brother has just married Lisa. Maya opened an Israeli kindergarten in Los Angeles. It is well known for its special Jewish Israeli character. All the children speak Hebrew, celebrate the Jewish holidays and sing Jewish and Israeli songs, and bake challot braided in honor of Shabbat! As I sat there with them, together yet alone with my thoughts, they wandered back to the most wonderful person I met, the father of my children, Leon (Lonek) Weinreb.

It was 1938. Lonek and I met for the first time at the annual Hanukkah Party at the Jewish school in Lwów, called the Jewish Gymnasium,

Leon (Lonek), Lala and Eli – 1958.

on 17 Zygmuntowska Street. I was very proud to have been chosen by him for the first dance. I had previously heard quite a lot about

him. He was a popular athlete and represented our school in various competitions. Lonek was very handsome, well liked and honored by all the students and teachers who knew him.

We enjoyed being together immensely and we had a very good time together. We spoke about many things and found we

Lonek's school, the Gymnasium.

shared common interests. It was then that he told me that his father was very active in Zionist groups and that their family often conversed in Hebrew at home. He told me his father intended to immigrate to Israel, then called Palestine.

Lonek's Hebrew was unusually good. When I mentioned to him that I would be happy to learn Hebrew, he suggested himself as my tutor. I thought it was a wonderful idea, and that it would be an opportunity for us to continue meeting and getting to know each other better. Soon his help became merely an excuse, because we fell in love.

When we were seeing each other, I asked him if I was his first love. He answered almost prophetically, "My first and last." As it turns out these were no idle words and it was like a promise which he would keep to the end of his life.

Our innocent happiness and courtship was soon marred by the upcoming conflict and events described my brother in Part One of this book.

All too soon the dreaded date of September 1939 arrived and with it the Second World War. German bombers began attacking Lwów. Quickly, we ran to take cover in a shelter.

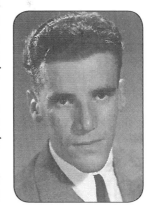

Lonek

Asaf & Lisa Betesh,
Maya's son, Lala's
grandson

Betesh family: Maya's son, Lala's
Grandson

Lala and her family with Grandson Eyal ben Ari

Lala and her grandchildren

Lala's daughter, Maya

Afraid to go out into the empty street, we waited until evening. That night the entire town was in complete blackout. Even the war could not keep us apart, and in spite of the conditions, we still managed to see each other every day.

On the 8th of September, Lonek descended nervously to our shelter, distraught, and with his voice trembling, he dropped a bombshell of his own. He said that his parents had made the decision to leave Lwów the very next day and escape by car in the direction of the Rumanian border.

My inner mood reflected the war going on outside and around me. As myriad thoughts raced through my mind, my emotions struggled like a storm within me. Questions pounded at me like shells hitting the ground splitting us apart! I could hardly talk. I was so overwhelmed.

The dreaded questions hung there in the air, with no answers: Was this then to be our final meeting? Was it goodbye forever? Would we ever see each other again? We both answered each other that we would meet again. We exchanged photos.

Lonek and his entire family were saved by "illegally" crossing the Rumanian border in a place called Zaleszczyki (pronounced Zaleshtcyki). Lonek received an affidavit from Rudi, his older brother who had years before settled in Palestine. He registered for the university in Jerusalem. They left Constance for Haifa in the Promised Land.

His life continued on as normal, while mine was shattered by the war. My fate was to suffer through the cruel years of the war and the Holocaust.

In May 1945, the war finally came to an end. From our family, once numbering some 43 persons, only 3 remained alive – my mother, my younger brother Julek and I.

And then . . .
Was it . . . DESTINY?
Was it . . . COINCIDENCE ?
Was it . . . A HIGHER POWER?

My grandfather Shlomo Greenfeld and his small family were living in Palestine, (pre-state of Israel). When they received the good news from the Polish Consulate that we were alive, they immediately sent for us, arranging all the necessary formalities, sending us precious certificates enabling us to be reunited with them.

Lala's son Eli ben Ari and his wife Michal

Lilach ben Ari, Michal & Eli's daughter

Tal ben Ari

Maya and Avi Betesh

On November 13, 1946, in Haifa my life returned more or less to normal. We got an apartment and restarted our family life, searching and locating opportunities to learn, study, and to work.

Lonek moved to Achad HaAm. By some miraculous coincidence unbeknownst to him, it was the very same neighborhood as that of my grandparents. He had Hebraicized his name to Arie.

One evening, while Lonek was looking over some photos of the past, from the days of our youth, he noticed something extraordinary – a photo of me. At that moment, the door bell rang and a neighbor and friend of the family, Dr. Weiss, entered. She asked him, "Is this Lala? By some miraculous 'coincidence' my cousins the Lippmans also have the same photo, but how do you happen to have it too?" In shock, he explained their previous relationship. She told him the most wonderful news that "Lala's grandfather is living on the same street as we do, and that his address is Achad HaAm number 78."

Beautiful flowers arrived at my grandfather's home. Attached was a little note which said, "Blessed be your arrival! Yours forever, Arie." We thought that we would never see each other again. The war and the cruel hand of fate tried to prevent our union. But it seems to me like some Higher Power intervened and was watching over us, making sure that we would be reunited.

The next day he appeared at my house. I thanked him for the flowers but without my usual characteristic smile. Before the war I had had a special smile. The war had erased it. He noticed this. When he questioned me asking "where had my characteristic smile vanished to?", I answered him that "I have forgotten how to smile." He answer me, "Don't be upset, in time it will return." At that time I did not believe him.

The first few days were difficult. We felt uneasy with each other. There was like a strange barrier that the war had erected between us. The burden of the terrible memories of my past lay heavily on me. I felt too grown up and too mature by those experiences. The years weighed heavily on my shoulders. This further estranged Lonek from me because of our very different wartime experiences.

Instinctively he understood me and felt my pain. Instead of taking me to the cinema and other forms of entertainment, we walked every evening on the seashore. The tempest staccato of the waves beating against the shore mirrored the turmoil of my heart. He begged me to talk about everything until late at night to re-live the burden of those cruel memories. The effect was cathartic and helped me heal. Only he felt my pain and he was there ready to listen.

All this was occurring during time of British Mandate. Lonek (Arie) was a member of the illegal and clandestine army known as the Hagana.

The Hagana was preparing the youth of Palestine for the inevitable struggle to free the land of our ancestors. From time to time Arie disappeared for few days to take part in the exercises which took place in the sand dunes of Holon.

Then in March of 1947, just two months before the outbreak of the War of Independence, Arie received a call from the Hagana to report to a placed called Tkuma in the Negev region. Their task was to guard the network of pipelines carrying water from the North to the Negev. This was a very dangerous assignment. If they were detected by the British Military, a confrontation would probably follow, ending with serious casualties on our side. The freedom fighters were ready to sacrifice everything for our independence and to free the land of our forefathers.

We exchanged letters, and Arie was always positive and hopeful. At last the day came for which we were waiting impatiently. His mission had been a success and Arie appeared, unannounced, in Tel Aviv. The meeting was very emotional as we reunited and together decided that from that moment on, we would not be separated again for the rest of our lives. We decided to marry. We announced our engagement to our parents. They were very happy and the next day they arranged an engagement party for the entire family.

For the occasion, Arie was awarded two days of extra leave from the Hagana – the two days that would save his life. Again a Higher Power intervened and was watching over us.

In the meantime his unit was transferred from Tkuma to Gush Etzion. By time he arrived to join his unit, he had received the tragic news that his comrades had fallen. They are eternally remembered as the Lamed Hay.

Our marriage was held in a small synagogue in Shivat Zion in May of 1948. Our lives together were happy. Our two children Eli and Maya were born. The atmosphere in our house was filled with friendship, understanding and youthful vitality.

Arie was active in many fields. He was a good pianist and joined the Philharmonic Orchestra as a member of the choir. He was an excellent sportsman, and a savior to people in distress. For example in 1951, there were great floods which threatened to overrun Jaffa. He mobilized his friends and together they rushed to save the residents. Everybody admired his novel character and so his friends gave him a nickname, Bedolach or "Crystal."

At the age of 45 his life was cut short due to illness. But his memory and his life's achievements live on for eternity.

I would like to share a poem[1] with you that touches my heart and symbolizes my feelings about the so-called coincidences of my life.

– Lala

Could Have

It could have happened.
It had to happen.

It happened earlier. Later.
Nearer. Farther off.

It happened, but not to you.
You were saved because you were the first.
You were saved because you were the last.

Alone. With others.
On the right. The left.
Because it was raining. Because of the shade.
Because the day was sunny.

You were in luck – there was a forest.
You were in luck – there were no trees.
You were in luck – a rake, a hook, a beam, a brake,
A jamb, a turn, a quarter-inch, an instant . . .

So you're here?

Still dizzy from another dodge, close shave, reprieve?
One hole in the net and you slipped through?
I couldn't be more shocked or speechless.
Listen – how your heart pounds inside me.

---

1   Wislawa Szymborska, "Could Have". This poem comes from her book, "View With a Grain of Sand" translated by Stanislaw Baranczak and Clare Cavanagh (New York: Harcourt, Brace, 1996).

Printed in Great Britain
by Amazon

43157209R00111